ARCHAEOLOGY
DETECTIVES

First edition for the United States and Canada published
in 2009 by Barron's Educational Series, Inc.

Text copyright © Oxford University Press 2008
Copyright © Oxford University Press 2008

All inquiries should be addressed to:
Barron's Educational Series, Inc.
250 Wireless Boulevard
Hauppauge, New York 11788
www.barronseduc.com

Library of Congress Control Number: 2008934725

ISBN-13: 978-0-7641-4273-4
ISBN-10: 0-7641-4273-9

Printed in China
9 8 7 6 5 4 3 2 1

ARCHAEOLOGY
DETECTIVES
Simon Adams

Uncovering the Past

BARRON'S

TABLE OF CONTENTS

WHAT IS ARCHAEOLOGY?

ARCHAEOLOGY IS DETECTIVE WORK IN TIME. LIKE DETECTIVES AT A CRIME SCENE, ARCHAEOLOGISTS EXAMINE EVIDENCE FROM HISTORY.

The word "archaeology" comes from the ancient Greek meaning "the study of what is ancient." Historians study old documents, while palaeontologists study fossils. Archaeologists study both of these, as well as many other sources of information—bits of pottery, tools and weapons, human remains, sunken ships, buried treasure, and the foundations of old buildings. You name it, they examine it! Every piece of material is studied to build up a picture of the past.

Archaeology can be hard, often unrewarding work. But every so often an archaeological detective will uncover a forgotten palace or buried tomb stuffed with priceless artifacts. Such finds make archaeology the most exciting form of detective work there is.

SCIENTIFIC TECHNIQUES

Archaeologists use a wide range of scientific tools and techniques to help them locate, excavate, examine, date, preserve, and display ancient remains. This Egyptian mummy is being given a computerized tomography (CT) scan. The scan uses X-rays and computer enhancement to examine the embalmed body without removing its outer linen wrapping.

Archaeologists find ancient towns and cities and sometimes uncover great treasures.

They discover lost civilizations and understand better how people lived in the past.

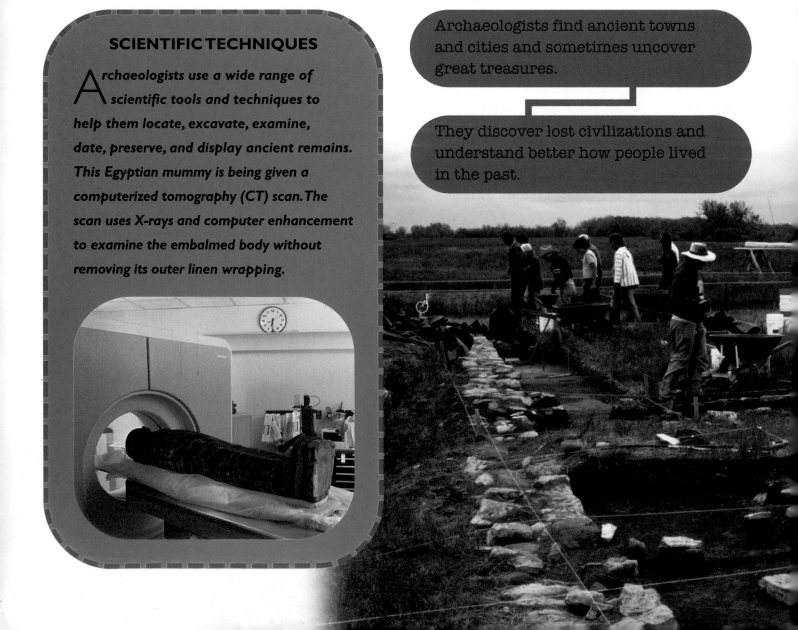

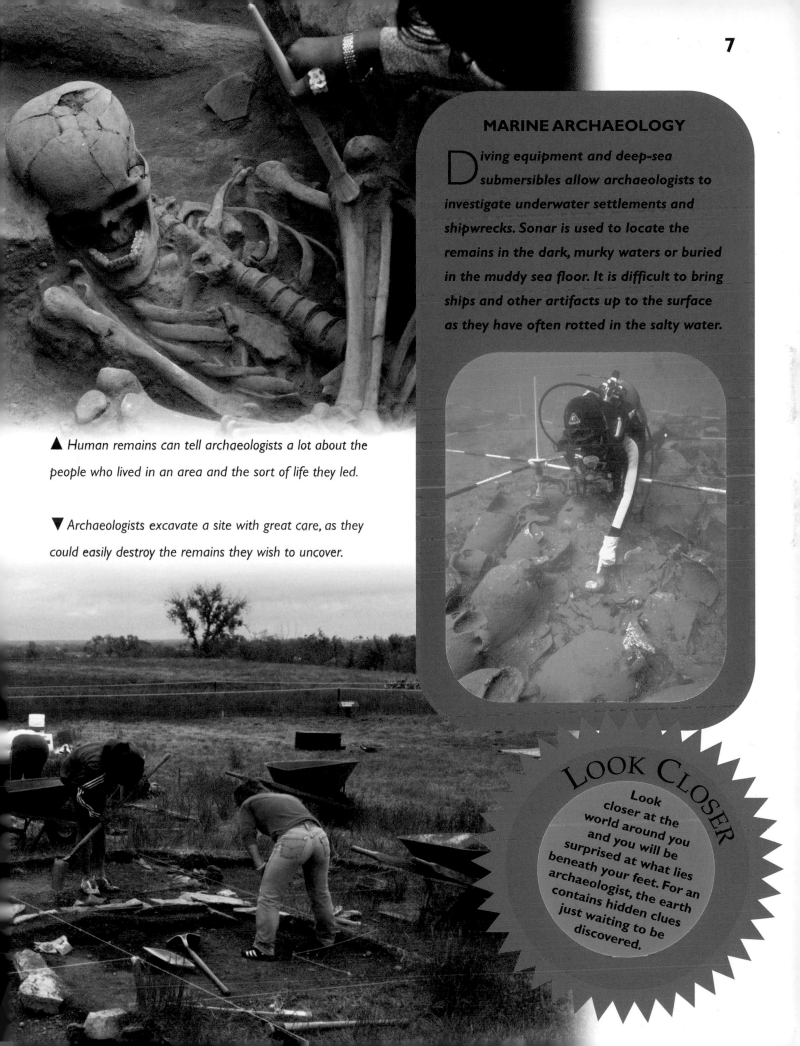

▲ Human remains can tell archaeologists a lot about the people who lived in an area and the sort of life they led.

▼ Archaeologists excavate a site with great care, as they could easily destroy the remains they wish to uncover.

MARINE ARCHAEOLOGY

Diving equipment and deep-sea submersibles allow archaeologists to investigate underwater settlements and shipwrecks. Sonar is used to locate the remains in the dark, murky waters or buried in the muddy sea floor. It is difficult to bring ships and other artifacts up to the surface as they have often rotted in the salty water.

LOOK CLOSER

Look closer at the world around you and you will be surprised at what lies beneath your feet. For an archaeologist, the earth contains hidden clues just waiting to be discovered.

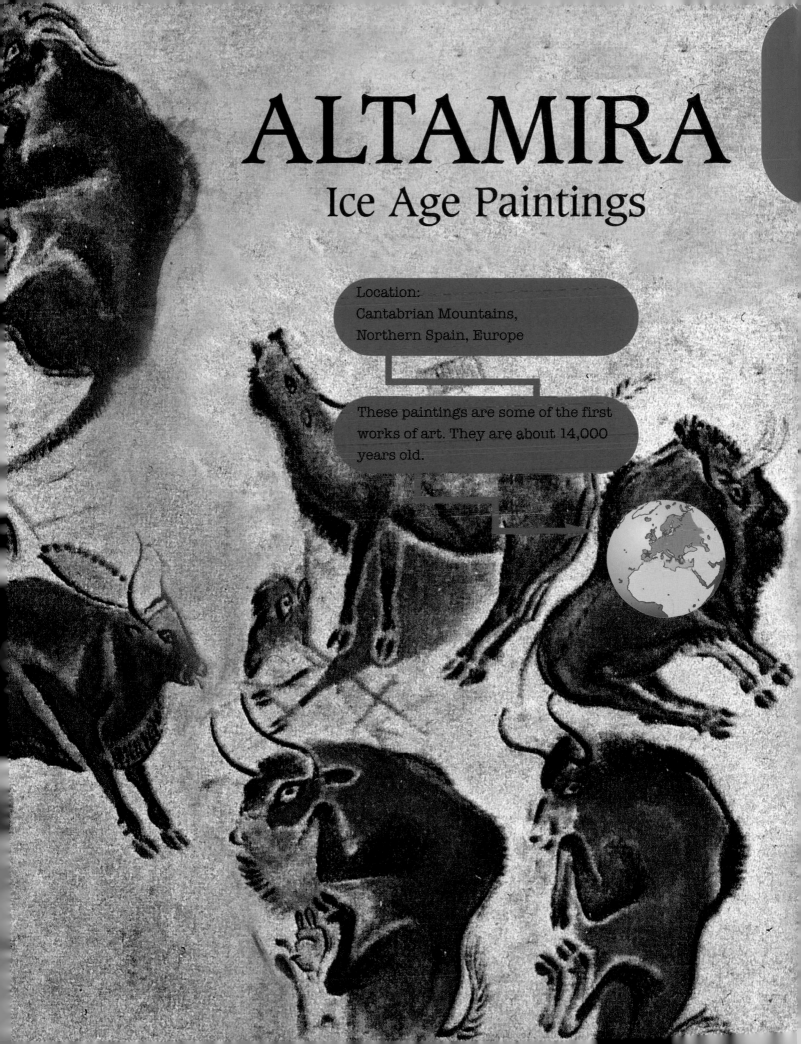

ALTAMIRA
Ice Age Paintings

Location:
Cantabrian Mountains,
Northern Spain, Europe

These paintings are some of the first works of art. They are about 14,000 years old.

THOUSANDS OF **YEARS** AGO, PEOPLE LIVED IN **CAVES.** THIS MIGHT SOUND **PRIMITIVE,** BUT THESE WERE NOT PRIMITIVE PEOPLE. THEY DECORATED THEIR CAVES WITH WONDERFUL **PAINTINGS.**

CAVE LIFE

IN THE DIM AND DISTANT PAST, ABOUT 14,000 YEARS AGO, THE PEOPLE IN NORTHERN SPAIN, LIKE OTHERS ALL OVER THE WORLD, LIVED IN CAVES.

These cave-dwellers lived in what we now call the Palaeolithic Age, a long period of time stretching from the appearance of earliest humans some three million years ago right up to about 8000 B.C. They lived right at the end of the last Ice Age, when temperatures were as much as 39°F lower than today. Caves provided warmth and shelter as well as protection from wild animals. Whole families lived together in one cave, preparing and cooking food on open fires, sleeping on animal skins, and painting on the walls.

PALAEOLITHIC PEOPLE

Life was hard for the Palaeolithic cave-dwellers. Their climate was harsh, and injuries killed many of them before the age of thirty. They did not know how to grow crops so had to hunt and gather whatever food was available. At that time, woolly mammoths strode the land. Catch one of these, and a whole family had enough meat to eat, skins to wear, and animal fat for making oil lamps for months.

▲ A woolly mammoth was a fearsome beast but it could be caught and eaten by hungry cave-dwellers.

◀▶ Tools and weapons were made by cutting and chipping away pieces of stone, flint, and bone to give them sharp cutting edges.

LOOK CLOSER

An ice age is caused by a major climate change that causes a massive drop in temperature. Snow and ice cover much of the ground, and glaciers form in valleys.

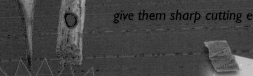

BACK TO THE CAVES

Luckily for archaeologists, cave-dwellers were not tidy. When they had finished with something, or broken it, they just dumped it in the back of the cave. Old flint tools, oil lamps, broken weapons, and bits of bone all piled up over the years. One cave in South Africa was probably only lived in for a couple of months a year, but the debris at the back piled up to 10 feet (3 m). This is rich evidence for archaeologists. It tells us a great deal about how cave people lived, all those thousands of years ago.

◀ Caves served as a home, workshop, and art gallery all in one place.

★ FROM A COLOR PRINT MADE IN 1900.

ICE AGE PAINTING

ALL THE CAVE PAINTINGS THAT HAVE BEEN FOUND IN EUROPE FEATURE ANIMALS PLUS A VERY FEW HUMANS AND SOME SIGNS.

When the first caves were discovered at the end of the 1800s, most people thought that the paintings inside were purely for decoration. More recently, archaeologists assumed that the paintings were to do with hunting magic or were perhaps fertility symbols.

Today, archaeologists are more concerned about where in the caves the paintings are placed. Larger paintings of horses and bison are usually in the center of the caves, while humans and dangerous animals, such as bears, are placed at the back of the caves or in side chambers. Most paintings are clearly visible but some are hidden away in inaccessible places.

▼ *Very few Ice Age cave paintings show people, but this painting from the Lascaux Caves in France pictures a wounded bison that seems to be attacking a man.*

Cave paintings depict a few types of animals. Horses and bison are most common.

People are shown in profile. No Ice Age paintings show vegetation or landscapes.

Surely there must be some reason for these paintings apart from simple decoration?

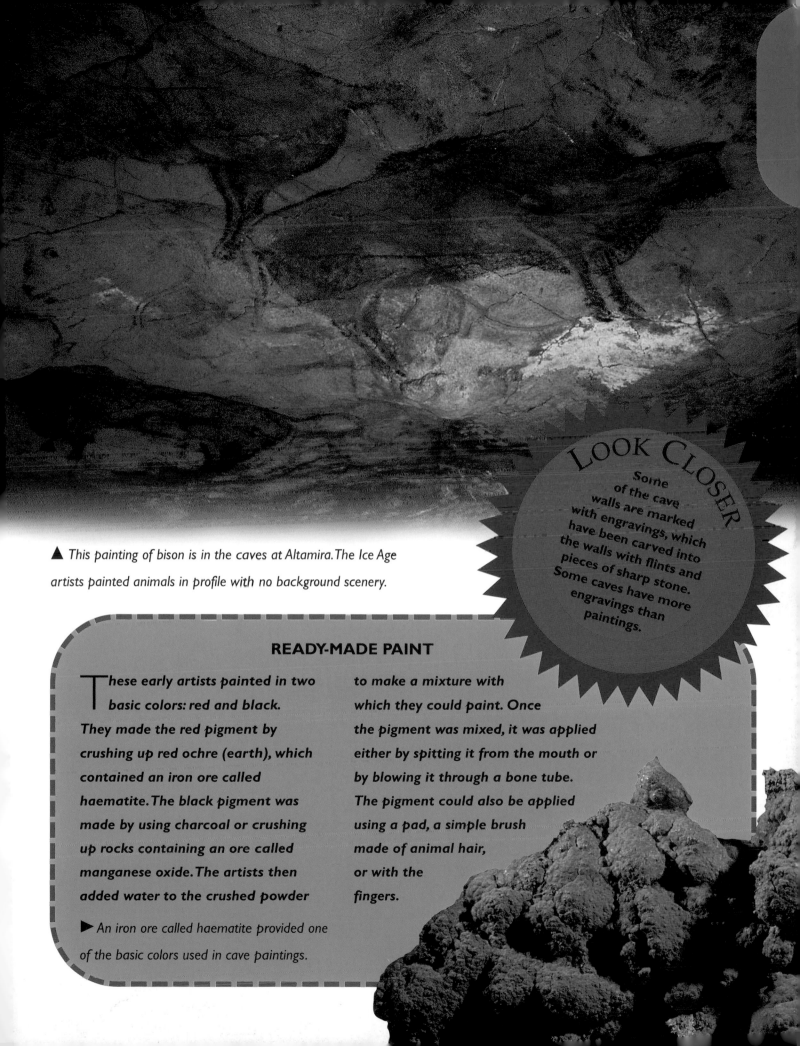

▲ This painting of bison is in the caves at Altamira. The Ice Age artists painted animals in profile with no background scenery.

LOOK CLOSER
Some of the cave walls are marked with engravings, which have been carved into the walls with flints and pieces of sharp stone. Some caves have more engravings than paintings.

READY-MADE PAINT

These early artists painted in two basic colors: red and black. They made the red pigment by crushing up red ochre (earth), which contained an iron ore called haematite. The black pigment was made by using charcoal or crushing up rocks containing an ore called manganese oxide. The artists then added water to the crushed powder to make a mixture with which they could paint. Once the pigment was mixed, it was applied either by spitting it from the mouth or by blowing it through a bone tube. The pigment could also be applied using a pad, a simple brush made of animal hair, or with the fingers.

▶ An iron ore called haematite provided one of the basic colors used in cave paintings.

CONTROVERSY!

PUBLICITY ABOUT THE PREHISTORIC PAINTINGS AT ALTAMIRA NEAR SANTANDER IN NORTHERN SPAIN CAUSED A MASSIVE CONTROVERSY AMONG THE LEADING ARCHAEOLOGISTS OF THE DAY.

Between 1875 and 1879, the local landowner, Don Marcelino de Sautuola, explored the 918 feet (280 m) deep caves and mapped their contents. He discovered red and black paintings of animals and some square signs, the meaning of which is still unknown. Some of the animals are up to 6.5 feet (2 m) across, with a spectacular group of bison, deer, and horses in a low hall near the entrance to the cave.

De Sautuola dated the paintings to between 13,000 and 11,000 B.C. The leading French archaeologist Gabriel de Mortillet did not think that prehistoric people could have produced such great art. It took twenty years for de Sautuola's theory to be accepted.

All the evidence in this cave shows that prehistoric people lived here 14,000 years ago.

If that is the case, they must have created these wonderful paintings, too.

LOOK CLOSE

De Sautuola examined flint tools and animal bones found near the entrance to the caves. These helped him date the paintings to the Palaeolithic period, around 14,000 years ago.

PRO-AM ARCHAEOLOGY

In 1864, Gabriel de Mortillet, the leading professional archaeologist of his time, founded Matériaux, one of the world's first archaeology journals. Don Marcelino de Sautuola (right) was an enthusiastic amateur. He suggested that the Altamira paintings dated from the Paleolithic period, but de Mortillet thought they were more recent. De Sautuola was even accused of faking the paintings. De Mortillet was later proved wrong and de Sautuola correct: a lesson to all archaeologists everywhere!

RADIOCARBON DATING

Modern dating techniques help avoid controversies like the dispute between de Sautuola and his critics. Radiocarbon dating was developed in 1949 as a way of dating organic matter, such as bones, skin, and wood. It is based on the fact that organic matter contains a tiny amount of the isotope carbon 14. The proportion of carbon 14 decreases at a constant rate after death. Carbon 14 reaches its halfway stage at 5,568 years, plus or minus 30 years. By measuring the amount of carbon 14 in an object, its age can be calculated. The method is reliable for dating objects up to 30,000 years.

▲ A scientist cleans a mammoth's tooth before radiocarbon dating it. Without circumstantial evidence, the tooth would otherwise be very difficult to date.

▼ This beautiful painting of a standing bison is in the caves of Altamira in northern Spain, first explored in the late 1870s.

MOHENJO-DARO
An Ancient Indian City

Location:
Indus River Valley,
Pakistan, Asia

One of the oldest cities and among the most advanced. It even had public bathrooms. WOW!

LONG FORGOTTEN

AND REDISCOVERED IN THE EARLY TWENTIETH CENTURY, THE CITIES OF THE INDUS VALLEY WERE ONCE HOME TO A CIVILIZATION THAT RIVALED THOSE OF EGYPT AND MESOPOTAMIA.

THE INDUS VALLEY

THE CITIES OF THE INDUS VALLEY WERE BUILT AROUND 2600 B.C. AT THE TIME, THEY WERE AMONG THE MOST ADVANCED URBAN AREAS IN THE WORLD.

The main cities of the Indus Valley—Mohenjo-Daro and Harappa—400 miles (644 km) northeast of Mojenjo-Daro—were built on a grid pattern, with houses at right angles to each other. Some of these houses were lavish in size and built around a central courtyard, while others were single-room properties. Each house had a bath and its own well, and most were connected to the city's main sewer. Among the public buildings were public baths and granaries sitting on underground air ducts to keep the grain from rotting.

▼ *The Great Bath in the center of Mohenjo-Daro was 39 feet (11.9 m) long and 23 feet (7 m) wide. It was built of brick and lined with asphalt.*

WHAT HAPPENED TO THE INDUS VALLEY?

There are many theories about what happened to the Indus Valley cities in 1900 B.C., when they were abandoned and fell into ruin. Perhaps the area was affected by movements in the Earth's crust as the Indian subcontinent moved toward the Himalayas. This caused the Indus River to change its course, depriving the cities of their main water supply. Another reason could be an outbreak of disease.

THE INDUS PEOPLE

The Indus Valley people could read and write, were skilled weavers, made crafts such as this model of a bird cage (left), made bricks of mud and straw, and irrigated the land to grow crops. We do not know much about their religion, but they probably worshipped a number of different gods and were ruled over by priest-kings (right).

LOOK CLOSER

The central location of the Great Bath suggests that it was used for ritual or religious purposes, perhaps to cleanse worshippers before entering a temple.

► This soapstone carving of a priest-king was found in Mohenjo-Daro.

GREAT BATH.

A LOST CIVILIZATION

WHEN MOHENJO-DARO WAS REDISCOVERED IN 1922, THE HISTORY OF THE ANCIENT WORLD HAD TO BE REWRITTEN.

The first archaeologists on the site began to excavate an ancient Buddhist temple dating back to the 200s B.C. Beneath its ruins they found a far older and more important ruin, that of a large Bronze Age city that no one had known existed. This was surprising, as the ruins are now in a semidesert area far from the nearest river. The archaeologists also found structures, such as the Great Bath, and icons on seals and other artifacts that link the religion of Mohenjo-Daro with the later Hindu religion of India. These links suggest that the roots of Hinduism may go back much farther than was originally thought. As a result of these discoveries, the social and religious history of the Indian subcontinent had to be revised.

▼ *The Mohenjo-Daro archaeological site in modern-day Pakistan was once home to the largest city and capital of the Indus Valley civilization.*

Archaeologists found ruins, but it is obvious that the buildings were once impressive structures.

Whoever built Mohenjo-Daro must have been extremely clever and highly sophisticated.

LOOK CLO

Mohenjo-Daro was a well-ordered city laid out in a grid pattern. The range of public and private buildings suggests that it was a wealthy society.

WRITING WITH PICTURES

The Indus Valley people traded goods as far away as modern-day Iraq. The goods were stored in large warehouses. In one warehouse in Harappa, archaeologists found more than 2,000 clay seals used by civic officials for stamping wax onto documents. The seals show about 400 picture signs. These signs have not yet been deciphered, and the language of the Indus Valley remains unknown.

REBUILDING THE WALLS

When archaeologists started to replace the broken mud and straw bricks of Mohenjo-Daro, they discovered that they were the same size as those used in the other valley cities. This suggests that the Indus Valley industry was highly regulated. Standard sets of weights and measures also suggest that this was an advanced civilization that controlled its economy to ensure wealth and prosperity.

SIR MORTIMER WHEELER

The British archaeologist Sir Mortimer Wheeler (1890–1976) developed a way of excavating a site in a regular pattern of squares or rectangles, leaving uninterrupted ground in between. This helped him to excavate at different levels across the site and then easily record his findings. This practice, called the Wheeler system, was perfected when Wheeler excavated the main granary at Mohenjo-Daro in 1950.

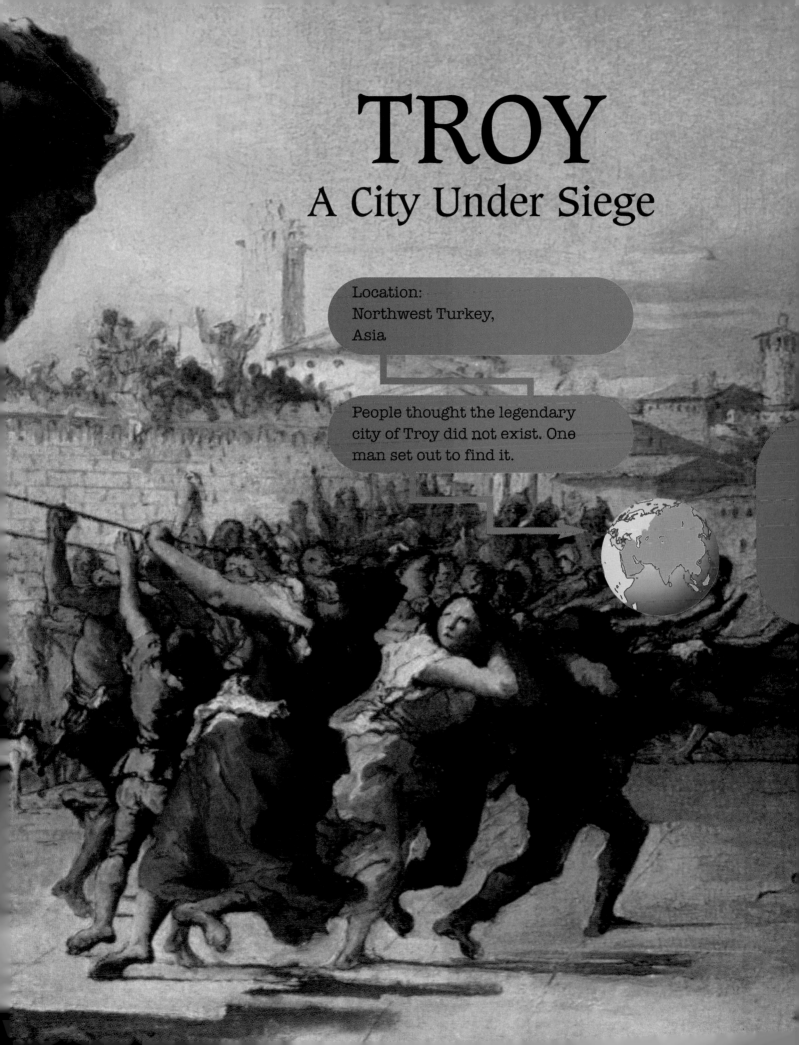

TROY
A City Under Siege

Location:
Northwest Turkey,
Asia

People thought the legendary
city of Troy did not exist. One
man set out to find it.

THE TROJAN WAR IS ONE OF THE MOST FAMOUS AND BELOVED OF ALL GREEK LEGENDS. CONTEMPORARY ACCOUNTS OF THE CONFLICT LED TO THE DISCOVERY OF THE CITY IN 1868 ON THE AEGEAN COAST OF TURKEY.

◀ *Great King Priam was the ruler of Troy. He had fifty sons, including Paris and Hector, and many daughters.*

THE TROJAN WAR

ACCORDING TO LEGEND, TROY WAS A MIGHTY CITY–STATE RULED BY KING PRIAM. THE CITY WAS DESCRIBED BY THE ANCIENT GREEK POET HOMER, IN HIS EPIC POEM THE *ILIAD*, WRITTEN ABOUT 2,750 YEARS AGO. HOMER TOLD HOW PRINCE PARIS, PRIAM'S SON, HAD RUN AWAY WITH HELEN, A BEAUTIFUL GREEK PRINCESS MARRIED TO MENELAUS, RULER OF SPARTA.

Menelaus and other Greek princes raised an army and sailed to Troy. They besieged the city for ten years. The siege ended when the Greeks tricked the Trojans. They pretended to sail away, leaving behind an enormous wooden horse as a gift to the gods. The Trojans took the horse into Troy. At night fully armed Greek soldiers crept out from inside the horse. They opened the gates of the city to let in a jubilant Greek army that then captured the city.

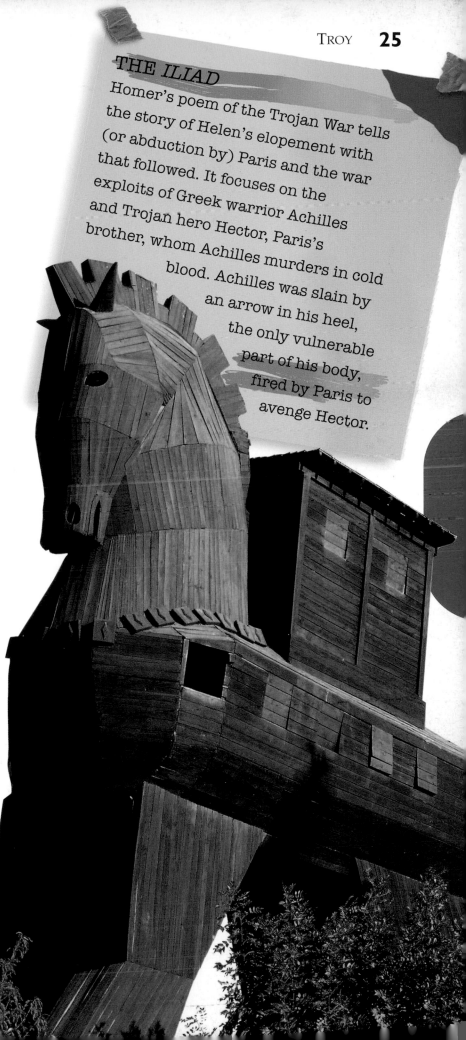

THE ILIAD

Homer's poem of the Trojan War tells the story of Helen's elopement with (or abduction by) Paris and the war that followed. It focuses on the exploits of Greek warrior Achilles and Trojan hero Hector, Paris's brother, whom Achilles murders in cold blood. Achilles was slain by an arrow in his heel, the only vulnerable part of his body, fired by Paris to avenge Hector.

▲ *Princess Helen and Prince Paris would have fled to Troy in a galley similar to this.*

Did Troy really exist? Heinrich Schliemann thought so.

Schliemann used the *Iliad* like a guidebook to locate Troy. Amazing!

▶ *A recent reconstruction of the mighty wooden horse of Troy.*

LOOK CLOSER

The story of the *Iliad* is not just an account of the war, but a tale of the anger, vengeance, and death of individual heroes.

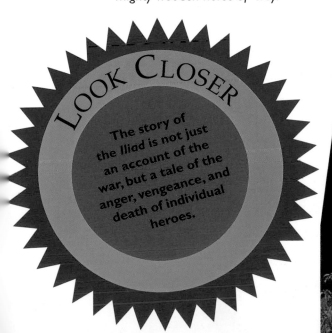

THE CITY OF TROY

FOR ALMOST 2,000 YEARS, THE CITY OF TROY FLOURISHED ON THE SHORES OF THE AEGEAN SEA. THE SITE SITS NEXT TO A PLACE CALLED HISSARLIK, IN MODERN-DAY TURKEY.

Troy began as a small farming village around 3000 B.C. Over the years, it grew rich on trade through the nearby Dardanelles between the Aegean and Black Seas. Archaeologists have discovered nine different layers to Troy, each built on top of the existing site. By the time of Troy VI, from 1900 to 1270 B.C., Troy was a wealthy city containing many public buildings.

Troy VI was destroyed, probably by an earthquake, in around 1270 B.C., but it was rebuilt as Troy VII. This city was destroyed around 1200 B.C. Either of these cities could have been destroyed by the Greeks at the end of the Trojan War. Around 700 B.C., the site was reoccupied by Greeks and later by the Romans. It fell into decline after 550 A.D. and was forgotten.

▼ Troy IX—the final settlement of the city—was built by the Romans around 133 B.C. They erected several fine buildings, including this open-air theater.

LOOK CLOSER

The nine layers of Troy sit on top of each other, but parts of each older city were built into its successor. Over the centuries, Troy rose up to become a large mound.

THE TROJANS

When Troy was first built around 3000 B.C., the entire area was populated by Stone Age farmers. Gradually, these people learned how to make bronze tools and weapons and developed a more sophisticated lifestyle. By 1500 B.C., the Trojans had built a wealthy city and were trading with the Mycenaean civilization of mainland Greece.

▲ An artist's reconstruction shows what Troy VI might have looked like around 1350 B.C. The city included many fine buildings and large warehouses used to store goods for trade.

Troy was obviously a mighty city that survived and prospered for many centuries.

In which case, it shouldn't be too difficult to find out what is left of it today!

THE APPEAL OF TROY

Troy has always excited the imagination. Around 750 B.C., the Greek poet Homer wrote his epic tale, the <u>Iliad</u>, about the last day of the Greek siege of Troy. His next volume, the <u>Odyssey</u>, recounts the wanderings of the warrior Odysseus after the Trojan War. In recent years, several films have been made about Troy and its famous siege, including one, in 2004, starring Orlando Bloom as Paris (right).

EXCAVATING TROY

HEINRICH SCHLIEMANN WAS OBSESSED WITH TROY. HE STARTED WORK IN 1871 AND CONTINUED UNTIL HIS DEATH IN 1890.

German businessman Heinrich Schliemann spent much of his later life excavating a mound at Hissarlik. He discovered that the mound was composed of many layers and that the second level from the bottom had been destroyed by fire. In its ruins he found more than 9,000 gold and silver objects. Schliemann was convinced that he had found Troy and with it the treasure of the legendary King Priam.

Schliemann thought if he started at the top and dug down, he would discover the city of Troy.

The city was set on fire and destroyed by the Greeks at the end of the Trojan War.

So if he found a burned city among the remains, he thought that it must be the legendary Troy!

▼ *Heinrich Schliemann was fascinated by Homer's tales and became an archaeologist to find out if the stories were true.*

STRATIGRAPHY

Archaeologists now use a technique called stratigraphy to study a multilayered site such as Troy. It helps them to work out how the site was formed, what it contains, in what order and timescale the different layers were laid down, and why some layers are thicker or thinner than others. Archaeologists once had to dig through the layers, possibly damaging their contents, but now they use a machine called a magnetometer to pick up changes in the underground magnetic field. This indicates the presence of ancient remains or artifacts.

WHAT SCHLIEMANN ACTUALLY FOUND

The ruins that Schliemann excavated were not the city of Homer's legend but were far older, dating back to around 2300 B.C. Of the nine layers that make up the site, Schliemann needed to excavate Troy VII, near the top, to find what he was looking for. In fact, the amateur archaeologist dug all the way down to Troy II, destroying the more recent remains as he did so. Schliemann was convinced he had excavated the right level and that the treasure he had found (including this gold earring) once belonged to King Priam. We now know that Schliemann was wrong, but his finds did a great deal to popularize archaeology and win it appeal.

LOOK CLOSER

These ruins at Troy (below) might look very old, but they are quite recent in historical terms. They date from the later Greek and Roman periods, well after the period of the Trojan War.

▼ Even archaeologists need to rest from the heat of the Sun, for excavating the ruins at Troy is always hard work!

PALACE OF KNOSSOS
The Minotaur's Palace

Location:
Northern Crete, Greece,
Europe

Is this the legendary palace with
an underground labyrinth where
King Minos lived?

THE MINOANS LIVED ON THE ISLAND OF CRETE IN THE AEGEAN SEA. THEY CREATED A CIVILIZATION 4,000 YEARS AGO WITH LAVISH ROYAL PALACES, ONE OF WHICH INCLUDED A LABYRINTH.

MINOAN CRETE

THE MINOANS CREATED AN ADVANCED CIVILIZATION ON THE GREEK ISLAND OF CRETE AROUND 2000 B.C. THERE, THE MINOANS RULED THEIR ISLAND FROM A SERIES OF ROYAL PALACES, OF WHICH THE MOST IMPORTANT WAS AT KNOSSOS.

The Minoans were skilled farmers and traders. Around 1700 B.C., most of the royal palaces were destroyed by fire, perhaps because of warfare between rival kings. The palace of Knossos was rebuilt and came to dominate Crete before it was damaged following a volcanic eruption on the nearby island of Thera in 1626 B.C. Once again the palace was rebuilt, but in 1450 B.C. the Minoan civilization came to an end when Mycenaean Greeks conquered the island.

MINOAN ARTS AND CRAFTS

The Minoans were skilled craftworkers. They were famous for their pottery vases, such as the one to the right—on display at the Iráklion Museum in Crete. Many Minoan vases feature the sacred labrys, or double-headed axe, which was an important religious symbol. Other vases depict octopuses and other sea animals. These creatures were important to the Minoans because they fished the seas for their food. The Minoans also produced tools and weapons made of bronze—tin and copper mixed together to make a harder metal—as well as woollen textiles. The Minoans traded their crafts for gold, ivory, and silver.

WRITING ON THE WALL

The origins of the Minoans remain unclear, as we cannot decipher their writing. At first, they wrote in hieroglyphs (pictures). By the 1700s B.C. they used a written script, which we call Linear A, in which each sign represented a syllable rather than a single letter. Neither of these scripts has been deciphered, but it is clear from them that the Minoans did not speak a European language, so they cannot be called Greeks.

LOOK CLOSER

The Minoans did not just live on Crete but all around the southern Aegean Sea. Their city of Akrotiri on Thera was preserved by ash when a volcano there erupted in 1626 BC.

▲ A Minoan priestess stands in ceremonial dress at an altar, offering a drink to the gods.

★ FROM A FRESCO DATING BACK TO THE FOURTEENTH CENTURY B.C.

THE ROYAL PALACES

The Minoan palaces were arranged around a central courtyard. The royal apartments were on the southeast side of the building to catch the cooling summer winds. These apartments had baths (right) with running water and other luxuries. The palaces also had large warehouses to store food that had been collected as tax or as gifts from subjects, as well as workshops for craftworkers.

THE LEGEND OF THE MINOTAUR

PASIPHAE, WIFE OF KING MINOS OF CRETE, FELL IN LOVE WITH A BULL SENT BY POSEIDON, GOD OF THE SEA. SHE GAVE BIRTH TO A HALF-BULL, HALF-HUMAN CALLED THE MINOTAUR. MINOS BUILT A LABYRINTH UNDER HIS PALACE TO HOUSE THE MONSTER.

According to legend, Theseus, the son of Aegeus, king of Athens, was set the task of killing the Minotaur. He sailed to Crete, where he fell in love with Ariadne,

Minos's daughter. She gave him a ball of wool, tied to the entrance, to guide him out of the labyrinth. Once inside, Theseus killed the Minotaur and then escaped from the labyrinth using the wool. He fled the island with Ariadne, but later married her sister, Phaedra.

The story of Theseus slaying the Minotaur is a popular legend of ancient Greece.

According to the story, the Minotaur lived in the labyrinth in the palace at Knossos.

▼ *Ariadne (left) gives Theseus a ball of wool to find his way back out of the labyrinth. Theseus (right) slays the Minotaur.*

KING MINOS

We do not really know if Minos—a king of Crete who dominated the Aegean Sea with his vast navy and ruled from his palace at Knossos—was a real historical figure or just a mythical character. What we do know is that the Minoan kings did have powerful navies and lived in huge palaces, decorated with the sacred labrys, after which a labyrinth is named. The story of Minos is so powerful that when the palace at Knossos was excavated, the civilization that built it was named Minoan in his honor.

LOOK CLOSER

In revenge for the murder of one of his sons in Athens, King Minos demanded that seven Athenian boys and seven girls be sacrificed every nine years to the Minotaur.

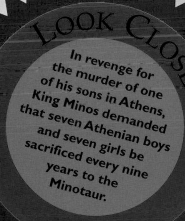

DAEDALUS AND ICARUS

The Athenian inventor Daedalus built the Minotaur's labyrinth. When the Minotaur was killed, Minos imprisoned Daedalus. But Daedalus escaped with his son, Icarus, by making wings of feathers and wax. When Icarus flew too close to the Sun, the wax in his wings melted and he crashed into the sea. Daedalus flew on to Sicily. His name became identified with any remarkable building or statue.

PALACE OF KNOSSOS

THE ENGLISH ARCHAEOLOGIST SIR ARTHUR EVANS BOUGHT A PLOT OF LAND NEAR IRÁKLION, CRETE, IN 1899. THERE, HE HOPED TO FIND THE TRUTH BEHIND THE LEGEND OF KING MINOS AND THE MINOTAUR.

In 1899, Evans uncovered the ruins of a palace dating back to between 2000 and 1400 B.C. The west wing of this vast palace was clearly a religious center devoted to bull worship. The more he excavated, the more Evans became convinced that this was the palace of King Minos, and that the story of the Minotaur was based on a religious cult. More importantly, Evans had uncovered evidence of an ancient civilization—the first great city–state in European history—that had existed more than 1,500 years before the ancient Greek civilizations of Athens and Sparta.

▼ Acrobats leap over the back of a large bull.

★ FROM A FRESCO AT THE MINOAN PALACE AT KNOSSOS.

LOOK CLOSER

The subjects worshipped the kings of Crete as bodily reincarnations of the bull god. This is why bulls played such an important part in Cretan religion.

RECONSTRUCTION

After excavating the site, Evans and his team of archaeologists rebuilt some of the ruins at Knossos to show visitors what the palace might have looked like when it was first built. Many people criticized Evans for this part of the work, particularly as he used modern materials such as reinforced concrete for the supporting pillars. This is always a problem for archaeologists: just how far should they go in their quest to bring the past back to life?

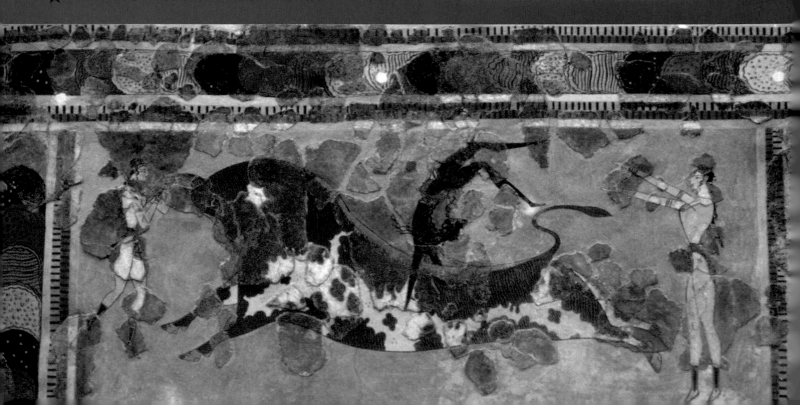

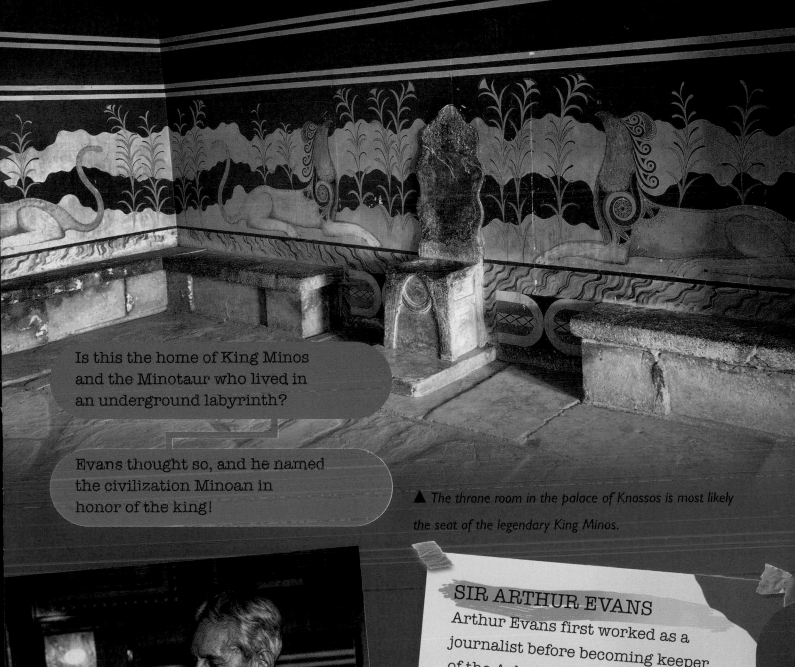

Is this the home of King Minos and the Minotaur who lived in an underground labyrinth?

Evans thought so, and he named the civilization Minoan in honor of the king!

▲ *The throne room in the palace of Knossos is most likely the seat of the legendary King Minos.*

SIR ARTHUR EVANS

Arthur Evans first worked as a journalist before becoming keeper of the Ashmolean Museum in Oxford, England. Study of ancient Greek seals led him to Crete. At his own expense, Evans began to excavate the palace of Knossos in 1899. He stayed in Crete for the next thirty-five years, using his family fortune to reconstruct much of the royal palace and the frescoes on its walls and thoroughly researching and excavating the ancient Minoan civilization.

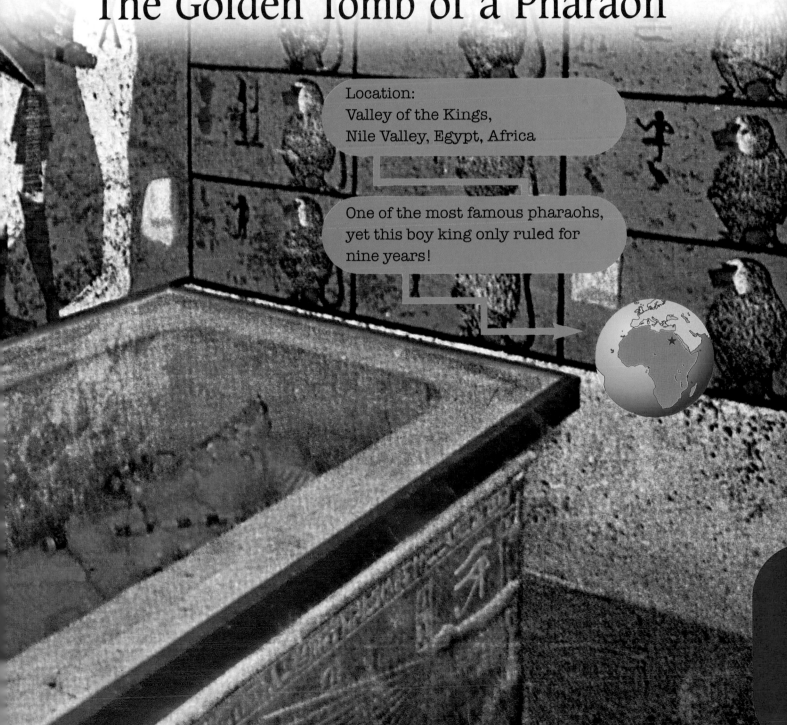

THE TOMB OF TUTANKHAMUN

The Golden Tomb of a Pharaoh

Location:
Valley of the Kings,
Nile Valley, Egypt, Africa

One of the most famous pharaohs,
yet this boy king only ruled for
nine years!

THE ANCIENT

EGYPTIAN

PHARAOHS

WERE WORSHIPPED

AS GODS AND

LIVED A LIFE OF

LUXURY AND

WEALTH. WHEN

THEY DIED, THEY

TOOK THAT WEALTH

WITH THEM INTO THE

AFTERLIFE.

▲ *The River Nile, the fertile lifeline of ancient Egypt.*

ANCIENT EGYPT

FOR ABOUT **3,000** YEARS, THE ANCIENT EGYPTIANS FLOURISHED ALONG THE BANKS OF THE RIVER NILE.

The first pharaohs (kings) of Egypt ruled around 2950 B.C. They built temples to worship their many gods and pyramid-shaped tombs in which they were buried. The Egyptians were a clever people. They developed picture writing called hieroglyphics to write down their religious scripts and laws. They also used the annual flood of the River Nile to irrigate their crops. Although ancient Egypt was frequently attacked by Greeks, Persians, and others, its civilization survived intact until the country eventually fell under Roman control in 30 B.C.

▶ *The Great Sphinx guards the pyramids at Giza. The early royal burial tombs were inside the pyramids.*

RELIGIOUS BELIEFS

The Egyptians worshipped many different gods and believed that their pharaoh was himself a god. They built huge temples (like the one at Luxor, right) to honor their gods, many of whom took the form of animals with human characteristics. The Egyptians believed their gods governed every aspect of daily life, from the rising of the Sun to the creation of life itself. They dreaded the idea that their world might one day cease to exist. They believed in an afterlife and hoped to live forever.

LOOK CLOSER

The Egyptians believed in magic. They devised a complex book of spells known as the Book of the Dead to help them through Duat—the underworld—into the next life.

This pyramid is a vast structure that appears to be built of solid stone.

But it must have been built for a purpose, perhaps to bury someone inside it?

That person must have been really important to get a tomb this big!

VALLEY OF THE KINGS

THE FIRST PHARAOHS WERE BURIED IN PYRAMIDS IN THE NORTH OF EGYPT. THESE VAST TOMBS WERE OFTEN RAIDED, HOWEVER, SO A SAFER, MORE REMOTE SITE WAS REQUIRED.

The Valley of the Kings lies in hills on the west bank of the Nile opposite the ancient capital of Thebes (Luxor) in the south of Egypt. From 1481 B.C. for the next four hundred years, almost every pharaoh was buried here. Sixty-two tombs have been discovered, along with twenty unfinished shafts and pits. Each tomb had a narrow doorway that led to a long, sloping tunnel. This opened out into a burial chamber deep inside the hill. Inside the chamber, the pharaoh was buried with everything he would need for the afterlife. The tunnel and the entrance were then filled with rubble to hide the tomb from grave robbers. However, most tombs were soon raided, leaving little of their precious contents behind.

LOOK CLOSER

The Valley of the Kings was an ideal burial site because it was so remote. It was easy to tunnel into the solid rock to create the network of tunnels leading to the tomb.

This hostile valley is just the place to bury a pharaoh and his treasure.

Most of these tombs have been stripped of their contents by grave robbers.

But could a tomb have survived unopened after all these years?

▲ A tomb was prepared in this valley for almost every pharaoh from Thutmose I (reigned 1493–1481 B.C.) to Rameses XI (reigned 1099–1069 B.C.).

▲ *Tutankhamun is shown in a garden with his wife, Queen Ankhesenamun.*

★ *FROM A CASKET.*

TUTANKHAMUN

Tutankhamun (shown with the goddess Nut) was born Tutankhaten, "perfect image of Aten," around 1340 B.C. His father Akhenaten worshipped Aten, the Sun-disc, as the only god. When Tutankhaten became pharaoh aged only eight or nine, he reinstated the old gods dominated by Amun, the king of the gods. He changed his name to Tutankhamun—"living image of Amun"—but only reigned for a decade before he died around 1322 B.C.

MUMMIFICATION

When a pharaoh died, the body was preserved for the afterlife. The organs were removed and the body covered with salt. The body was then wrapped in linen bandages to form a mummy. This was placed in a wooden coffin inside a stone sarcophagus that stood in the center of the royal tomb.

DISCOVERY

ALMOST ALL THE TOMBS IN THE VALLEY OF THE KINGS HAD BEEN FOUND, BUT MOST WERE EMPTY. EGYPT SPECIALIST HOWARD CARTER BELIEVED THAT ONE TOMB REMAINED— THAT OF TUTANKHAMUN.

Sponsored by his rich patron, Lord Carnarvon, Carter began to excavate. On November 1, 1922, he uncovered a group of huts used by the workmen who had built the tombs. A flight of twelve steps under one of the huts led to a sealed doorway. Carter had found the tomb.

▼ *Carter and his associate examine the innermost, solid-gold coffin containing the mummified body of Tutankhamun.*

TOMB OF TREASURES

On November 26, 1922, the tomb entrance was cleared. "Can you see anything?" asked Lord Carnarvon. "Yes, wonderful things," replied Carter. The tomb was packed with beautiful gold and alabaster ornaments, ornate games and model boats, decorated furniture such as chairs and footstools, and other priceless objects, all dating back some 3,250 years. Inside the burial chamber, Tutankhamun's mummified body was found covered with gold jewelry and precious stones. The tomb of an ancient pharaoh had finally been discovered intact.

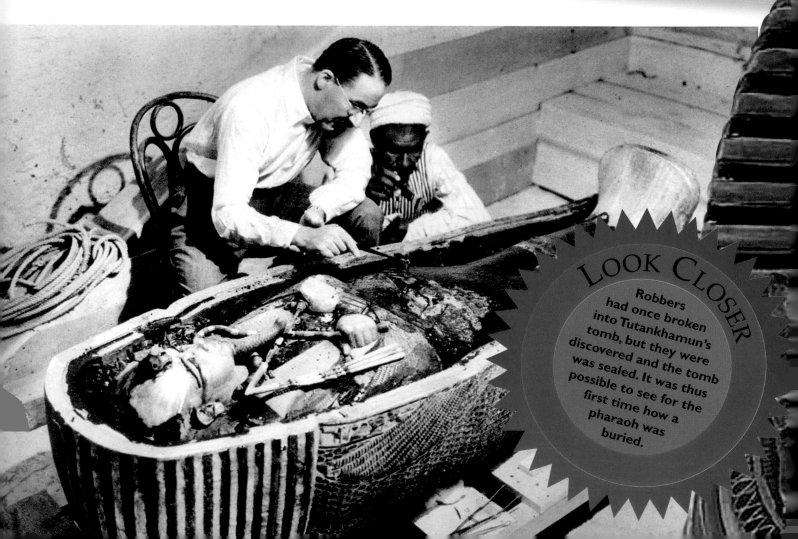

LOOK CLOSER

Robbers had once broken into Tutankhamun's tomb, but they were discovered and the tomb was sealed. It was thus possible to see for the first time how a pharaoh was buried.

THE CURSE OF THE MUMMY

Four months after Tutankhamun's tomb was opened, Lord Carnarvon died in Cairo. Some people blamed the mummy for his unexpected death. They believed that the dead pharaoh placed a curse on those who had entered his tomb. This curse has since been blamed for the deaths of many people associated with the tomb. The reality is that there is no curse—all the deaths can be explained naturally.

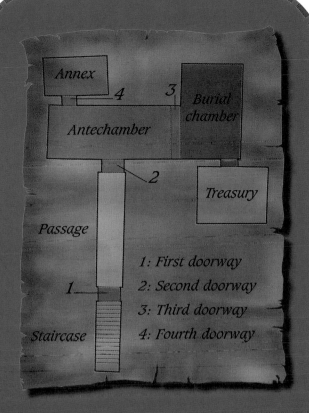

Annex

4

3

Burial chamber

Antechamber

2

Treasury

Passage

1: First doorway

2: Second doorway

1

3: Third doorway

4: Fourth doorway

Staircase

INSIDE THE TOMB

Tutankhamun's tomb consists of a long passage leading to an antechamber. A small annex leads off to one side, with the main burial chamber and treasury to the right. Sealed doorways blocked up the different rooms. As the contents of the tomb were relatively undisturbed, they told us not just how a pharaoh was buried but also about how the ancient Egyptians lived.

This is the gold mask of Tutankhamun, the young pharaoh of ancient Egypt.

Thanks to Howard Carter, we know more about Tutankhamun than any other pharaoh.

MONT LASSOIS AND VIX

Celtic Hill Fort and Burial Site

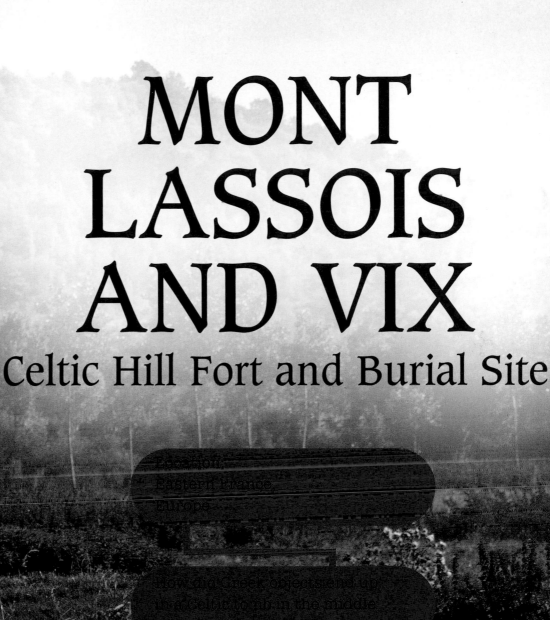

Location:
Eastern France,
Europe

How did Greek objects end up
in a Celtic tomb in the middle
of France?

FROM THE SIXTH CENTURY B.C., A FLOURISHING TRADE IN LUXURY GOODS AND RAW MATERIALS GREW BETWEEN THE GREEKS AND CELTS THAT WAS TO BENEFIT BOTH SIDES.

THE CELTS

THE CELTS PROBABLY ORIGINATED IN THE ALPS IN CENTRAL EUROPE. THEY DID NOT KEEP WRITTEN RECORDS, SO LITTLE IS KNOWN ABOUT THEM. BUT WE DO KNOW THAT THEY WERE FIERCE WARRIORS AND SKILLED BRONZE-, AND LATER, IRON-WORKERS.

The Celts spread out over much of central and western Europe after 1000 B.C. They traded with the Greeks and other maritime peoples of the Mediterranean Sea. It was Greek writers who first called these people Celts; the Romans called them Gauls. The Celts were governed by powerful chieftains, who built hill forts to protect themselves and their families from their enemies. One of these hill forts was constructed at Mont Lassois in eastern France.

CELTIC WARRIORS

The Celts were great warriors, attacking their enemies with ferocity and ranging far across Europe in search of wealth. Celtic tribes sacked Rome in 390 B.C. and got as far south as Delphi in Greece in 279 B.C. Later they crossed into Asia and raided central Turkey. The Celts fought with swords and spears, such as this iron spear with bronze supports found in the River Thames in England. But they were not invincible. They suffered defeat by the Romans in France in 52 B.C. and were later threatened by Germanic tribes from northern Europe.

CELTIC ART

The Celts developed a distinctive style of art known as La Tène art. Craftworkers made clay heads of warriors or gods (left) that were used in religious rituals or to protect the tribe from evil spirits. They made bronze shields that were offered up to the gods, as well as gold models of sailing ships, gold and silver jewelry, and bronze and iron weapons, such as spears and swords, for their warriors.

▼ The Celts built hill forts across north and west Europe, including this impressive structure at Danebury in England, occupied between the sixth and first centuries B.C.

LOOK CLOSER

Hill forts consist of rings of defensive ramparts and ditches circling a flat area. On this were granaries, storage pits, and living huts. The fort's entrance was through a single gateway.

CELTIC TRADE

THE HILL FORT OF MONT LASSOIS WAS THE HOME OF A POWERFUL CELTIC CHIEFTAIN. IT OWED ITS IMPORTANCE TO ITS POSITION ON ONE OF THE MOST IMPORTANT TRADE ROUTES IN WESTERN EUROPE.

The Celtic world was rich in raw materials such as cereal grains, metal ores, and slaves captured in war. The Greeks produced goods such as wine, pottery, jewelry, and other luxury items. Each group wanted the other's goods, so a lucrative trade developed.

Mont Lassois was one of the main trading centers. Greek traders traveled from the Mediterranean coast up the Rhône and Saône Rivers to Mont Lassois. Celtic traders traveled down the Seine Valley from northern Europe. The trade brought great wealth to Mont Lassois and its chieftains.

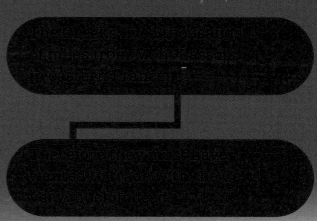

GREEK TRADERS

After 900 B.C. the Greeks set up trading colonies around the Mediterranean and Black Seas. Soon the Greeks came into conflict with another seagoing trading people—the Phoenicians from Carthage in North Africa. The Phoenicians could not stop the Greeks from establishing a major colony near the mouth of the Rhône in Massilia (now Marseilles) around 600 B.C. It was from there that the Greek traders would have set off northwards toward Mont Lassois.

▼ Greek trading ships were powered by a single sail with a double-oared rudder at the stern. Some ships had a row of oars on either side to drive them forward in light winds or power them along a river.

LUXURY TRADE

We can get a good idea about the trade between the ancient Greeks and Celts from some of the artifacts found at Mont Lassois. Artifacts have also been recovered from the tomb of a high-ranking woman in the village of Vix, directly below the hill fort (see pages 52–53). Brooches and other items of Greek jewelry as well as metalware and pottery were unearthed. Pottery finds included pieces of amphorae, which were used to store wine and olive oil. The quality of these pieces indicates both the wealth and high status of the hill fort's occupants and the long-distance trade they were engaged in.

▲ Distinctive Greek black-figure pottery and a bronze jug with a bronze basin from one of the Etruscan city–states discovered in the tomb at Vix.

A CELTIC BURIAL

OVER THE YEARS, MANY CELTIC BURIAL MOUNDS HAVE BEEN FOUND NEAR MONT LASSOIS. THE MOST SPECTACULAR WAS FOUND IN 1953 IN THE VILLAGE OF VIX.

The burial mound was 138 feet (42 m) across and 20 feet (6 m) tall. Inside was a rectangular wooden chamber. It contained the body of a princess lying on a wooden cart and surrounded by bronze wagon fittings. Alongside the body were items such as jewelry and utensils, which she would need for the afterlife. The most impressive object was a large bronze krater (wine mixing bowl). Dating of these grave goods indicated that the young princess was buried at some time between 520 and 500 B.C.

THE AFTERLIFE

Like the ancient Egyptians, the Celts believed in an afterlife and buried the dead with all the items they would need to survive in the next world. The princess at Vix was buried with a cart for transport; decorative jewelry; basins, jugs, and cups to hold her food and drink; and a bronze krater in which to mix her wine. The high quality of these items indicates that the woman inside the tomb was of noble birth.

THE JEWELS OF A PRINCESS

Among the jewels the princess was buried with was this solid gold torque, or necklace. Weighing 17 ounces (.48 kg) and adorned with winged horses, this torque was made either in Greece or Italy. Solid gold bracelets, a brooch, and many more torques accompanied her to the afterlife. The princess was also buried with two Greek cups and a bronze basin from Etruria—the Etruscan homeland. The origin and quality of these goods give us a good idea about the scale of Celtic–Greek trade at the time.

LOOK CLOSER

Women played an important role in the Celtic world. One of the most famous is Boudicca, queen of the Iceni tribe in England, who fought against the Romans in the first century A.D.

THE VIX KRATER

The most important find in the Vix burial chamber was a massive bronze krater. The krater was 66 inches (167 cm) tall and weighed 459 pounds (208 kg). The neck was decorated with an embossed frieze of soldiers and chariots. The krater was held with two ornate handles cast in the shape of gorgons—winged monsters with snakes for hair. The Vix Krater was made in Sparta in Greece or in the Greek colony of Tarentum in southern Italy. It probably arrived at Mont Lassois in pieces, where it was put together by a skilled Greek craftsman. We know this because each section of the krater is clearly numbered in Greek.

◄ One of the handles of the massive Vix Krater can be seen emerging from the ground. The krater remained hidden in the burial chamber for almost 2,500 years.

Imagine excavating a Celtic burial mound and not knowing what you might find.

And then uncovering this giant bronze krater buried deep beneath the soil. WOW!

Unearthing stunning artifacts such as this is what makes archaeology so exciting!

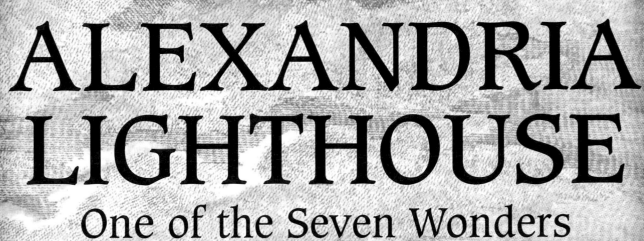

ALEXANDRIA LIGHTHOUSE

One of the Seven Wonders of the Ancient World

Location:
Alexandria, Nile Delta,
Egypt, Africa

WOW! Modern technology
located an ancient wonder
under a modern harbor.

THE GREAT CITY OF

ALEXANDRIA

WAS FOUNDED BY

THE MACEDONIAN

ALEXANDER

THE GREAT.

HIS CONQUESTS LED

HIM THROUGH

EGYPT AND

PERSIA

INTO INDIA.

ALEXANDER

ALEXANDER (356–323 B.C.) WAS THE SON OF KING PHILIP II OF MACEDONIA AND PRINCESS OLYMPIAS, THE DAUGHTER OF THE KING OF ANOTHER GREEK STATE, EPIRUS.

Alexander's parents were powerful people who wanted their son to follow in their footsteps. He was educated by all the best possible teachers of the day, including the philosopher Aristotle. Alexander was only sixteen when Philip made him regent of Macedonia while he was away fighting in a war against the Persians. When his father was assassinated (some say Alexander was involved) he became king at the age of nineteen. Having conquered and subdued all of Greece, Alexander set out to civilize the whole known world.

BUCEPHALUS

Some say that the great love of Alexander's life was his horse, Bucephalus. The horse was given to King Philip, but nobody could ride him. The twelve-year-old Alexander claimed he could. Philip said that Alexander could have the horse if he could ride him. Alexander had noticed that the horse shied away from his own shadow. He led Bucephalus into the sun, where the shadow was behind him. Alexander was able to mount, and the horse was his. The two rode many thousands of miles together. Bucephalus was given a state funeral when he died.

ALEXANDER THE GREAT— THE MOVIES

Such a short, powerful, and romantic life is bound to be food and drink to Hollywood. Several films have been made. Sadly the subject has usually overwhelmed the filmmakers! In 1956, Richard Burton tried to conquer. Unbelievably, in a TV version in 1968, Captain Kirk himself, William Shatner, attempted the role. In the latest film, released in 2004, the conqueror was played by Colin Farrell (see above).

◀ Alexander and Bucephalus fought in many battles together until the horse died of battle wounds in India.

★ DETAIL FROM THE ALEXANDER MOSAIC AT THE HOUSE OF THE FAUN IN POMPEII, ITALY.

LOOK CLOSER
Among the earliest surviving accounts of Alexander were those of his greatest general, Ptolemy I Soter. He became ruler of Egypt and made Alexandria his capital.

CONQUERING THE WORLD

FROM 336 TO 323 B.C., ALEXANDER
CONQUERED MOST OF THE KNOWN
WORLD AND CREATED ONE OF THE
GREATEST EMPIRES OF ANCIENT TIMES.

When his father Philip of Macedon was killed in 336 B.C.,
Alexander became king and united the many Greek kingdoms
under his rule. In 334, he invaded Asia and won a battle with
mighty Persia. He then conquered Egypt in 332, and defeated
the Persians again in 331, before invading central Asia in 329.
When Alexander died in 323, his empire stretched from Greece
in the west to modern-day Pakistan in the east, and from Egypt
in the south to central Asia in the north.

◄ Amun was the king of the
gods. Alexander wanted his
powers to become godlike and
associated himself with Amun.

NAMING CITIES

In 340 B.C., when Alexander was
just sixteen, his father King Philip
of Macedon made his son regent
(temporary ruler) of the country
while he was abroad. Alexander
wanted to see some military action,
so he organized an army to attack
the Maedi people on Macedonia's
eastern border. After he defeated
the Maedi, Alexander created a new
Greek-style city on the site of their
former capital. He named it
Alexandroupolis, and it was the
first of perhaps twenty cities he
created and named after himself.
The most famous of these is
Alexandria in Egypt, founded in
331 B.C.

ALEXANDER THE GOD

When Alexander was in Egypt in 331 B.C., he went on
a journey into the desert to consult the oracle of Amun—
the king of the gods—at the Siwah oasis. No one knows why
Alexander visited the oracle, or what questions he asked. What
is known is that after the visit Alexander always claimed a close
relationship to Amun and perhaps believed that Amun was his
father. The Egyptians worshipped Alexander as a god because
he was now their pharaoh or ruler, and every pharaoh was
divine. Later in life, Alexander made his subjects pay homage
to him as if he were a living god.

◀ *A coin shows Alexander with the ram horns of Amun, the god he believed to be his father, as Amun was a vigorous god. Alexander's conquests changed the world forever.*

ALEXANDER'S LEGACY

Alexander left a vast empire after his death but no obvious heir. By 270 B.C., his empire had split into Egypt, Macedonia, and Persia. Yet Greek culture and language dominated, helping Christianity to become a major world religion. St. Paul, the main apostle, spoke Greek, and the New Testament was first written down in Greek. Alexander's legacy lives on today.

▼ *Alexander defeats the Persians in Egypt. The city of Alexandria is born.*

★ *FROM A FIFTEENTH-CENTURY FLORENTINE PAINTING.*

LOOK CLOSER

Alexander died in Babylon, Iraq, but was finally buried in his new city of Alexandria. The city has since been rebuilt many times, and his exact burial site has never been discovered.

ALEXANDER'S CITY

AFTER ALEXANDER DIED, ALEXANDRIA WAS COMPLETED BY PTOLEMY I SOTER. THE CITY BECAME RICH AND WAS THE CENTER OF THE CIVILIZED WORLD. IT NEEDED A SYMBOL AND LIGHT TO GUIDE SHIPS INTO THE HARBOR.

In 290 B.C. the building of the Pharos Lighthouse began. It was the first lighthouse in the world and stood for nearly 1,500 years but was destroyed in an earthquake in 1303 A.D. In 2004, archaeologists unearthed more than 2,000 blocks of stone in the harbor at Alexandria. Near the blocks lay several stones that may have decorated the lighthouse.

▲ *The lighthouse became one of the seven wonders of the ancient world.*

★ *A VICTORIAN PAINTING OF THE PHAROS LIGHTHOUSE.*

LOOK CLOSER

The fort of Qaitbey was built in the fifteenth century where the Pharos once stood. Some of the lighthouse stones were used in the fort's walls.

The Pharos stones on the seabed were marked with floating masts.

Measurement stations on shore and satellites could map their exact positions.

The information was computerized to create a database of the sea floor.

Modern technology tracked the ruins of technology from the third century B.C. WOW!

▲ Many artifacts found on the seabed need painstaking reconstruction.

PRESERVING THE REMAINS

Water is a fertile environment for archaeologists. Saltwater preserves natural materials like wood by stopping them from interacting with oxygen. However, they often begin to rot when they are removed from the sea. Constantly keeping the objects wet helps to preserve them. An alternative is to slowly replace the water with a plastic-type resin that soaks into the wood and hardens, sealing it from the air. Stone or granite is not affected by the sea, although weeds and sea creatures may have made their homes in the remains.

▼ Scuba-diving archaeologists find all sorts of ancient objects on the ocean floor.

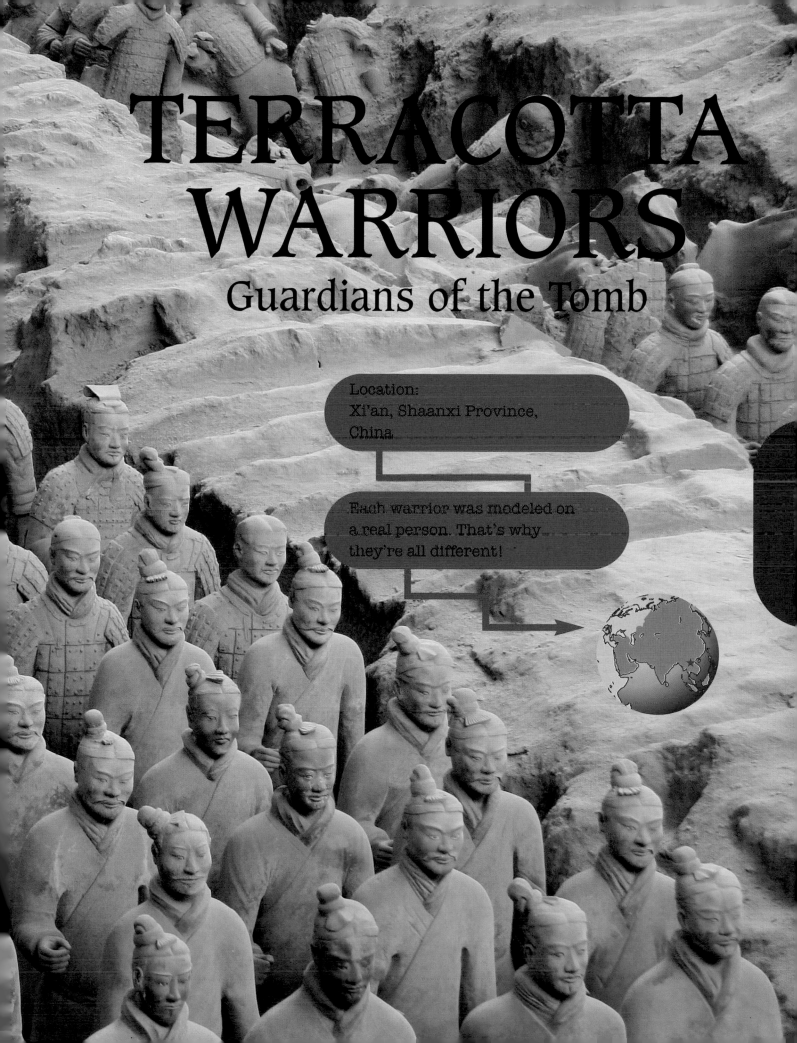

TERRACOTTA WARRIORS

Guardians of the Tomb

Location:
Xi'an, Shaanxi Province,
China

Each warrior was modeled on
a real person. That's why
they're all different!

KING ZHENG

OF THE QIN

KINGDOM UNITED

CHINA FOR THE

FIRST TIME AND

BECAME ITS FIRST

EMPEROR.

HIS RULE WAS GREAT,

BUT HE WANTED TO

CONTINUE HIS LIFE

AFTER DEATH.

THE FIRST EMPEROR

ZHENG, KING OF QIN STATE IN WESTERN CHINA, WAS A FEARSOME WARRIOR. IN 221 B.C. HE UNITED ALL THE WARRING STATES UNDER HIS RULE. HE NAMED HIS NEW EMPIRE QIN— PRONOUNCED CHIN, OR CHINA.

Zheng was a very able ruler, imposing a common Chinese script throughout the country and standardizing weights and measures. He started a major building program, including the Great Wall and many new roads and canals.

The emperor wanted to live forever after death. As soon as he became emperor, he began to plan a magnificent tomb guarded by terracotta soldiers who would protect him in his afterlife.

DISUNITED CHINA

Ancient China was not a single state like it is today, but a collection of small unruly kingdoms loosely held together. The Shang kings ruled much of northern China from about 1650 to 1027 B.C., but they were more like priests than monarchs. The Zhou dynasty that followed was a little more effective, but powerful nobles constantly rose up against it. By 481 B.C. China had split into seven warring states. They fought huge battles using armored infantry, chariots, and crossbowmen. More than half a million men were killed in one battle in 260 B.C. So great was the chaos that General Sun Tzu wrote a book, _The Art of War_, telling armies how to fight better.

始 秦

LOOK CLOSER

Some people say you can see the Great Wall of China from space. You can't—unless you have a very powerful telescope—but you can see it from an airplane!

THE GREAT WALL

Many of the warring states of China had built earth walls around their borders and cities. When the first emperor unified China, he tore down many of these walls. He kept some to create a long wall along the north of China to keep out warring nomads. That wall was built of earth. The stone wall we see today was not built until much later.

PREPARING FOR DEATH

ZHENG BECAME KING OF QIN IN 246 B.C. PREPARATIONS FOR HIS DEATH TOOK ON A MASSIVE SCALE WHEN HE BECAME THE CHINESE EMPEROR IN 221 B.C.

Zheng was obsessed with immortality. He took potions to prolong his life and he built a huge burial mound to protect his body in the afterlife. To guard this mound, Zheng built a funeral palace and a temple and dug a series of at least four large pits covering around 275,000 square feet (25,548 sq m). The pits were paved with 250,000 clay bricks and covered with wooden roofs. Standing in the pits is a life-size army of terracotta warriors.

Zheng became ruler of the Qin kingdom when he was just thirteen years old.

When he became emperor of the united empire, Zheng changed his name to Qin Shi Huangdi.

The new name means the First Sovereign Qin Emperor in honor of his new role.

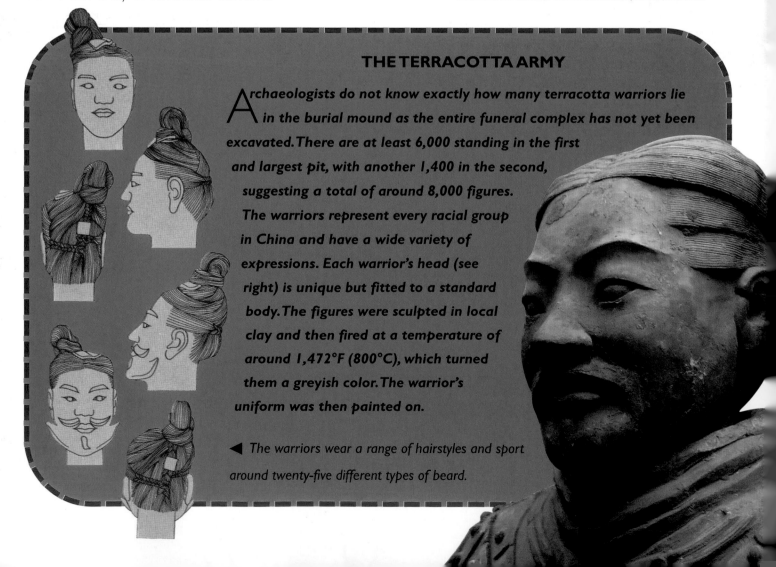

THE TERRACOTTA ARMY

Archaeologists do not know exactly how many terracotta warriors lie in the burial mound as the entire funeral complex has not yet been excavated. There are at least 6,000 standing in the first and largest pit, with another 1,400 in the second, suggesting a total of around 8,000 figures. The warriors represent every racial group in China and have a wide variety of expressions. Each warrior's head (see right) is unique but fitted to a standard body. The figures were sculpted in local clay and then fired at a temperature of around 1,472°F (800°C), which turned them a greyish color. The warrior's uniform was then painted on.

◀ The warriors wear a range of hairstyles and sport around twenty-five different types of beard.

THE BURIAL MOUND

*Z*heng's burial mound lies some 0.9 miles (1.4 km) to the west of his guardian terracotta army. The squarish mound is 165 feet (4.9 m) high. It has never been excavated. According to contemporary accounts, it contains booby traps of loaded crossbows and other weapons to protect the emperor, while rivers of mercury flow around the tomb. In 2007, archaeologists using remote-sensing equipment discovered a 98-foot (29.8-m) tall building buried deep inside the mound.

► At least 600 horses and 100 chariots accompany the 8,000 soldiers in the tomb.

LOOK CLOSER

The names of eighty-five sculptors are engraved under the armpits or beneath the long coats of the warriors. The sculptors obviously wanted to be remembered for their work.

▼ The walls that separate the rows of warriors from the burial mound were built by tamping earth between wooden frames.

DISCOVERING THE TOMB

IN 1974, WORKERS WERE DIGGING A WELL NEAR XI'AN IN SHAANXI PROVINCE. THEY FOUND THE TERRACOTTA HEAD OF A GENERAL, WITH SOME TERRACOTTA ARMS ENTANGLED IN ANCIENT BAMBOO MATTING.

As more heads and bodies were uncovered, the vast scale of the site and its extraordinary contents soon became clear. The first and largest pit extends 755 feet (230 m) from east to west and 203 feet (61.8 m) from north to south. It is divided into eleven corridors, separated by walls of tamped earth. Five large earthen ramps lead up to the surface. The other three pits are smaller but no less impressive. These workers had found the Eighth Wonder of the World!

The first Qin emperor was one of the most powerful and feared men in the world.

When he died in 210 B.C., he took the secrets of his burial mound to his grave.

The mound remains undisturbed, apparently protected by the emperor's fearsome reputation.

▼ *The emperor's burial mound is surrounded by two walls and planted with pomegranate trees.*

NEW FINDS

Archaeologists are still excavating the funeral site. In recent years, they have found the graves of human beings with severed limbs, bronze chariots, suits of armor, and replica weapons made from limestone. They have also found terracotta figures of acrobats, artists, musicians, and scribes. As new parts of the tomb are uncovered, we are learning more and more about the first emperor and the mighty empire he conquered and ruled.

LOOK CLOSER

It took 700,000 conscripts more than twenty years to build Qin Shi Huangdi's grand burial mound, and thousands more to dig the funeral pits and fill them with soldiers.

▲ *Archaeologists painstakingly record the details of each warrior, where he was found, and the condition he is in.*

TERRACOTTA JIGSAW PUZZLE

Many of the terracotta statues still lie under the ground and require careful excavation and restoration. Some of the figures are in one piece while others are broken into many pieces and need fixing back together again! Chinese archaeologists have only excavated around 1,000 of the estimated 8,000 soldiers at the burial site. Many of the treasures unearthed from the funeral pits are on display at a museum built next to the site, which attracts millions of tourists every year.

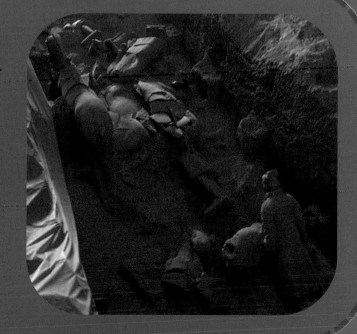

THE ROSETTA STONE

Cracking an Ancient Code

Location:
Rosetta, Nile Delta,
Egypt

A stone that held the key to
understanding the language
of an ancient civilization.

THE ANCIENT EGYPTIANS HAD AN ALPHABET BUT NOT ONE WE WOULD RECOGNIZE TODAY. THEY WROTE IN PICTURES AND HAD AT LEAST 1,000 DIFFERENT SIGNS FOR THEIR WORDS.

PICTURE LANGUAGE

THE ANCIENT EGYPTIANS DEVELOPED A COMPLICATED PICTURE LANGUAGE KNOWN AS HIEROGLYPHICS. THEY USED IT FOR MORE THAN 3,000 YEARS.

When the Greek Ptolemy dynasty ruled Egypt after 305 B.C., they introduced the Coptic script. This used mainly Greek letters, and the old hieroglyphs fell out of use. In the 600s A.D., the Arabs invaded and had their own Arabic script. By then nobody could write or understand hieroglyphics.

LOOK CLOSER

Hieroglyphics used pictures called hieroglyphs to represent sounds and meanings. It could be written from left to right, right to left, or from top to bottom.

► This young scribe is sitting cross-legged with a papyrus scroll in his lap, ready to start writing.

EGYPTIAN WRITING

The main form of writing was hieroglyphics, a complicated picture language used on tombs, temples, and religious documents. The everyday script for business and letters was called hieratic. It was simpler and faster to write. In about 600 B.C., an even simpler form, called demotic, was developed.

THE SCRIBES —SKILLED WORKERS

Scribes were near the top of Egyptian society. They trained from the age of nine for at least five years. They learned a skill that few other Egyptians could master. Scribes wrote on clay tablets or on paper made from the papyrus reeds (above) that grew along the banks of the River Nile. They used thin reed brushes dipped in ink. Some scribes worked as sculptors, carving hieroglyphs into stone or wood. Others painted hieroglyphs onto plastered tomb or temple walls.

THE STONE

IN 1798, FRENCH TROOPS COMMANDED BY NAPOLEON BONAPARTE ARRIVED IN EGYPT TO EXPAND THEIR EMPIRE TO THE EAST.

In July 1799, troops began to rebuild the walls of a fort near the town of Rosetta. They found a curious stone of dark grey polished granite. The stone had three languages on it. The one at the bottom was easy to read—it was ancient Greek. The other two were hieroglyphics and demotic. Nobody could read what they said.

▼ *French soldiers sought out ancient remains like mummies and sarcophagi (the stone chests protecting coffins) to study or take home as trophies!*

THE STORY OF THE STONE

After the stone was discovered, it was taken to the Egyptian capital, Cairo, for study. The Greek script at the bottom was a decree issued on March 27, 196 B.C. It honored the coronation of the pharaoh Ptolemy V. Copies of the stone were made and sent to Paris. Scholars tried to work out what the hieroglyphs meant, but none succeeded. In 1801, the British took control of Egypt. The stone was handed over to them.

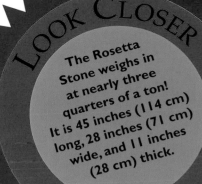
► In 1802, the Rosetta Stone was brought to London, where it has been ever since. It is now on display in the British Museum in London.

★ THE ROSETTA STONE IN THE BRITISH MUSEUM, LONDON.

ROYAL WRITING

This temple wall shows two pharaohs, the king and queen of ancient Egypt. We know they are pharaohs because they are wearing royal crowns. Above them are five columns of hieroglyphs. Columns two and three are written inside an oval frame called a cartouche. Because the pharaohs were so important, their names were always written inside a cartouche.

◄ The names written inside the cartouches on this temple wall are royal names.

CRACKING THE CODE

THE CODE WAS FINALLY BROKEN BY A FRENCH SCHOLAR, JEAN-FRANÇOIS CHAMPOLLION. WHEN HE STARTED TO DECIPHER THE STONE, HE THOUGHT HIEROGLYPHICS WAS A PICTURE LANGUAGE AND EVERY SIGN REPRESENTED A WORD.

Champollion knew that royal names appeared in cartouches and recognized the words for "temple" and "Greeks." He realized hieroglyphic script was not a picture language. It was more like an alphabet, like the one we use today. Most of the pictures and signs represented a sound, just as "a" and "b" do to us. He proved this by looking at the name Ptolemy on the stone. Ptolemy has seven letters in Greek, and there were seven signs in the cartouche. The code was cracked at last!

THE CODE-BREAKER

Jean-François Champollion (1790–1832) was a brilliant linguist. He had learned more than a dozen languages by the time he was eighteen and was a university professor at nineteen! He was fascinated by ancient Egypt, and he was determined to read and understand hieroglyphs. Using a copy of the stone, he slowly solved the puzzle. He announced his results in 1822. Two years later he published the first ever book of ancient Egyptian grammar.

THE KEY TO THE SECRET

This page from Champollion's grammar book shows how he made his breakthrough. The three cartouches are the names of the pharaohs Ptolemy (marked 1), Cleopatra (5), and Berenice (16). He worked out that the square in the upper right-hand corner of Ptolemy's cartouche was the hieroglyph for P. The hieratic sign for P is shown at 4. The lion and the hieratic sign at 7 both mean L. Champollion worked his way through the hieroglyphic and demotic writing on the stone, using his knowledge of ancient Greek as his guide.

◀ A page from Champollion's book, published in 1824.

LOOK CLOSER

Champollion deciphered the writing on the Rosetta Stone, slowly but surely, using his knowledge of languages. Today's code-breakers use high-speed computers instead!

▲ Parts of the Rosetta Stone are broken. Champollion (left) needed to study other inscriptions as well.

Champollion read ancient Greek, so he could understand the bottom of the stone.

He recognized the first two scripts as being hieroglyphic and demotic.

By comparing the scripts he could work out what they meant.

POMPEII
Roman City

Location:
Southern Italy,
Europe

This city was once a thriving port and trade center. How did it end up in ruins?

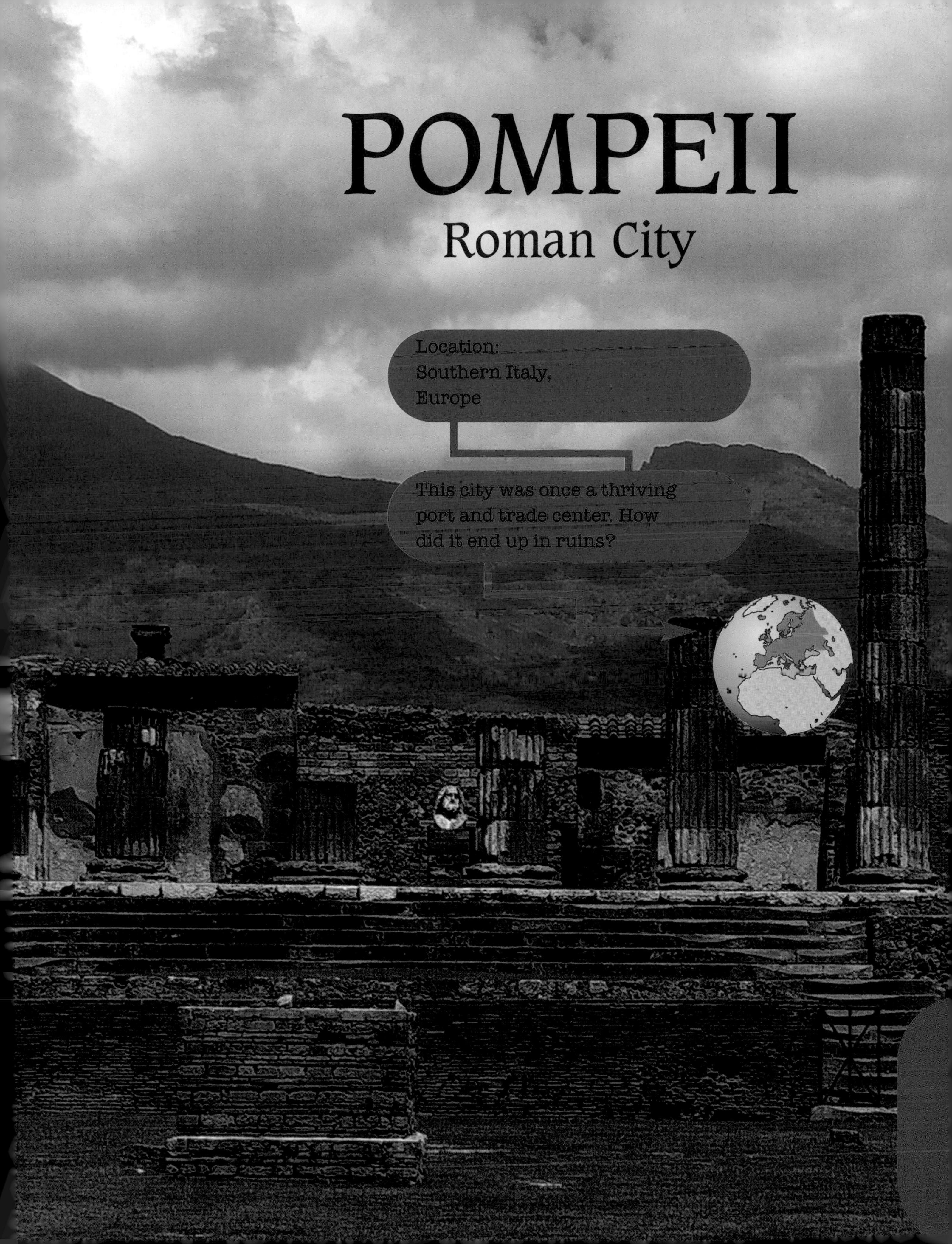

IN 79 A.D. A VOLCANO ERUPTED NEAR THE ROMAN TOWN OF POMPEII. THE VOLCANO BURIED THE TOWN UNDER MOUNTAINS OF LAVA AND ASH, PRESERVING IT FOR 1,700 YEARS.

▲ When heavy rain flooded the streets, the large stones in the middle of the road allowed pedestrians to cross without getting wet but allowed wheeled vehicles to pass without hindrance.

A ROMAN TOWN

POMPEII LIES ON THE BAY OF NAPLES IN SOUTHERN ITALY. IN 79 A.D., A FREAK ACT OF NATURE MADE POMPEII ONE OF THE MOST FAMOUS OF ALL ROMAN TOWNS.

Pompeii was a rich, bustling port that made its money from the surrounding agricultural lands. Traders exported olive oil, wine, and other products across the Mediterranean Sea, while its workshops made and sold pottery, metalwork, and other items. The town itself was surrounded by walls and contained many fine public buildings, such as the forum and the senate house, linked by wide, paved roads.

For entertainment, the citizens of Pompeii could visit the large amphitheater, which held 20,000 spectators. The town also had two theaters—a large, 5,000-seater for entertainments and a small, 1,000-seater for more artistic performances. Three public baths were fed by water from the great Aqua Augusta aqueduct.

ROMAN EMPIRE

Rome was founded around 753 B.C. In 510 the Romans declared a republic. Over the next 500 years, the Roman republic expanded across the whole of Italy. It eventually dominated the lands around the Mediterranean Sea. After a period of dictatorship and civil war, Augustus became the first emperor of Rome in 27 B.C. By 117 A.D. the Roman empire was at its height, controlling western Europe, North Africa, and much of the Middle East. After repeated attacks by tribes from central Europe, the Roman empire collapsed in 476 A.D.

▼ *Corn was ground under this millstone before being turned into bread and cooked in the brick oven behind.*

LUXURY LIVING

Rich Pompeii merchants lived in huge villas decorated with wall paintings, filled with fine furniture, and built around a central, open-air atrium. One of the most splendid villas was the Vettis' House. This villa contained an apartment with a porch reserved for the women of the house, while the servants lived in their own two-story quarters. A colonnaded courtyard at the back contained cooling fountains and was filled with statues and flowering and aromatic plants. There the family kept cool during the hot summer months.

LOOK CLOSER

In many houses in Pompeii, the rooms facing the road doubled as shops and workshops to make clothes or furniture, bake bread, or sell food, wine, and other items.

ERUPTION!

COVERED WITH GREEN WOODS AND VINEYARDS, MT. VESUVIUS LOOKED LIKE ANY OTHER MOUNTAIN. NO ONE REALIZED THAT IT WAS A VOLCANO; THERE WAS NO HISTORICAL RECORD OF IT EVER HAVING ERUPTED BEFORE.

The morning of August 24, 79 A.D. was just like any other summer's day, but gradually the sky grew dark. Mt. Vesuvius exploded with massive force, throwing out molten lava and clouds of ash and gas that rained down on the unsuspecting people below. As they tried to escape from the erupting volcano, the hot ash made them cough and sputter. Eventually they succumbed to the heat and ash and were buried where they lay. Within a few days, the town was buried in a 20-foot (6 m) blanket of ash that preserved it almost intact for more than 1,700 years.

▼ *As Vesuvius erupts, Pliny the Elder urges his family and his nephew to flee.*

★ *FROM AN ENGRAVING BY ANGELICA KAUFFMANN.*

LOOK CLOSER

Pliny the Elder sailed to Pompeii as the volcano erupted. He died inhaling fumes. His nephew, Pliny the Younger, recorded the events in letters to the historian Tacitus.

Ash from Vesuvius covered every building in Pompeii and killed thousands of people.

Could some of these buildings remain preserved in the ash after all these years?

MT. VESUVIUS

Until the eruption of 79 A.D., Mt. Vesuvius had been dormant for more than 800 years. Since then, the volcano has erupted with increasing frequency, notably in 1631 and again in 1767, 1779, and 1885. In this picture (left), the fishermen are using light from an eruption in the early 1800s to attract fish at night. Tourists still flock to Mt. Vesuvius despite the danger to their lives if the volcano chose to explode again .

VOLCANOES

A volcano is a gap in the Earth's crust through which ash, gas, molten lava, and other materials escape to the surface. Volcanoes come in many shapes and sizes. Most have a crater or vent at the top through which these materials escape. An active volcano is one that erupts regularly or could erupt at any moment. Currently there are about 1,300 active volcanoes on land throughout the world, as well as many more on the sea floor. A dormant volcano is one that has been inactive for centuries but can erupt suddenly —just like Vesuvius in 79 A.D. An extinct volcano is no longer likely to erupt.

POMPEII UNCOVERED

POMPEII LAY UNDISTURBED AFTER THE ERUPTION, AND THE TOWN WAS ALMOST FORGOTTEN UNTIL EXCAVATION BEGAN IN 1748.

Most Roman towns fell into disuse after the empire collapsed in the late 400s or were substantially rebuilt in subsequent years. Despite the damage the volcano caused, Pompeii is complete and unaltered. Archaeologists have excavated almost the entire town. As a result, we are now able to go back in time and see how and where the Romans lived and what they did in their lives.

▲ *A bowl of eggs was discovered intact in Pompeii, preserved after the eruption.*

No one could have survived the eruption, so their bodies must still be buried in the ash.

Is it possible to dig them up and learn something about how and where they died?

▼ *Archaeologists extract the plaster casts of the bodies of two adults and three children from the ashy ground of Pompeii.*

PAINTING LIFE

Many wall paintings and mosaics survive in Pompeii's houses and other buildings. They show in great detail what the Romans looked like and how they lived. The fresco on the right was once thought to be of the famous Greek poet Sappho. Historians now think she is more likely to be a well-dressed member of the family that owned the house.

▶ Many of the plaster casts show that the victims of the volcano died a horrible death. Some show their faces wracked with fear. Other people tried to hide or find shelter under a roof or in a cellar.

LOOK CLOSER

Fiorelli's plaster cast technique is still used whenever a new body is found at the site. It has also been used to make casts of animals, trees, doors, furniture, and cartwheels.

GIUSEPPE FIORELLI

In 1860 the Italian king appointed Giuseppe Fiorelli as director of excavations at Pompeii. Fiorelli began the first systematic excavation of Pompeii, painstakingly recording his findings. One gruesome discovery was the remains of more than 2,000 people who died as a rain of ash set hard around them. Over the years, the fleshy body parts decayed, leaving a hollow cavity containing only their bones. Fiorelli perfected a method of extracting the bones and filling the cavity with plaster. When the plaster hardened, he dug the cast of the body out of the solid ground.

TENOCHTITLÁN
Capital of the Mighty Aztec Empire

Location:
Under Mexico City,
Mexico, Central America

This city was once home to
250,000 people. How did it
disappear without a trace?

IN A LITTLE LESS THAN 200 YEARS, THE AZTECS OF MEXICO CREATED A FABULOUS BUT BRUTAL EMPIRE CENTERED AT THEIR CAPITAL OF TENOCHTITLÁN IN THE MIDDLE OF LAKE TEXCOCO.

THE AZTECS

THE AZTECS CAME FROM THE NORTHERN DESERTS OF MEXICO BUT MOVED SOUTH IN 1325, BUILDING TENOCHTITLÁN, THEIR CAPITAL, ON LAKE TEXCOCO.

Originally, the Aztecs occupied a small area of land next to Lake Texcoco. In 1434 they formed an alliance with two of their neighbors and soon dominated the whole of the Central Valley of Mexico. By 1500, the Aztecs ruled over 10 million people and controlled central Mexico, from the Pacific Ocean to the Caribbean coasts.

The Aztec state was governed by an all-powerful emperor whose subjects worshipped him as a god. The Aztecs worshipped many other gods and goddesses. Elaborate rituals were performed to keep these gods happy so that the Sun would shine and the rain would water their crops.

HUMAN SACRIFICES

The Aztec army used spears (two gold-plated ceremonial spears are shown at right) to force subjects to pay tribute to the emperor. This tribute took the form of gifts of precious items such as gold as well as human sacrifices. The unfortunate victims were taken to the Templo Mayor (Great Temple) in Tenochtitlán and had their hearts ripped from their chests as a gift to the Sun god Huitzilopochtli. The scale of the sacrifice was vast— up to 20,000 prisoners were killed in a single four-day ceremony.

QUETZALCÓATL

Legend has it that the Aztec god Quetzalcóatl ("feathered serpent," whose shell-encrusted turquoise mask is shown at left) was a fair-skinned and bearded god who once fled his kingdom because he had quarreled with another god. Quetzalcóatl vowed one day to return to his kingdom. When the Spanish arrived in 1519, the Aztec emperor feared that the fair-skinned and bearded conquistadors might be the returning Quetzalcóatl. As a result, the Aztec army refused to fight the invaders.

▼ *Moctezuma II was the last Aztec emperor. He ruled his empire from 1502 until his death in 1520.*

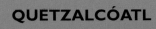

RISE AND FALL

Hernan Cortés landed on the Mexican coast in 1519 with 400 soldiers, 15 horsemen, and a few hundred porters. Within two years he had conquered the Aztec empire. The Spanish had the advantage of guns, armor, and horses, none of which the Aztecs possessed, but they also had allies. The Aztec practice of human sacrifice meant that 100,000 subjects joined the Spanish forces to fight against their former masters.

In 1519 Tenochtitlán was a city of 250,000 people and contained many buildings.

Surely something of a city of this size and splendor must still exist today!

TENOCHTITLÁN

Tenochtitlán, the ancient capital of the Aztecs, was built on an island in the middle of Lake Texcoco. The city was home to around 250,000 people—more than any European city of its day.

The center of Tenochtitlán was dominated by a walled precinct containing the Templo Mayor (Great Temple). Four large, wide, straight streets divided the city into four quarters, which contained many fine palaces, state buildings, and private houses. Reclaimed swampland from the lake was used to grow beans, chillies, maize, squash, and other crops needed to feed the capital's growing population. A levee protected these marshes from the salt waters of Lake Texcoco, where many salt-making stations were located.

▼ *This illustrated map of Tenochtitlán is said to have been drawn by Hernan Cortés himself and gives a good impression of scale and grandeur of the city.*

LOOK CLOSER

European maps of Tenochtitlán clearly show the city divided into four quarters. These were the basis on which taxes were raised and men called up for military service.

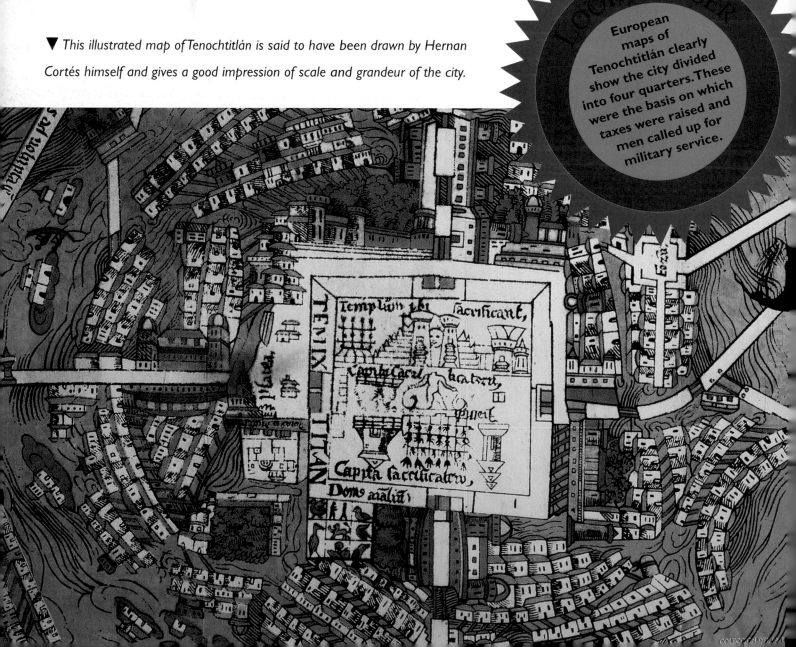

▼ Aztec people mill around the ceremonial center of Tenochtitlán. The double temple–pyramid of the Templo Mayor is at the left of the picture.

THE AZTEC UNIVERSE

The Aztecs thought that the universe had passed through four creations, which had been destroyed before the fifth and most recent universe began. The Sun, Moon, stars, and people were created at the start of this fifth universe, which the Aztecs thought would be destroyed by earthquakes. This Sun stone shows the Sun god surrounded by the four previous universes and a gold band on which is inscribed the twenty days of each sacred calendar month.

THE TEMPLO MAYOR

The Templo Mayor was a tall pyramid topped with twin shrines to the gods of rain and war. The temple was the religious center of the Aztec empire. It was used to make offerings and human sacrifices to the gods. The Aztecs believed that the world would end if they did not make these offerings, the most important of which was human blood. Each emperor made the temple bigger and more impressive, building around and on top of the previous temple.

UNCOVERING HISTORY

THE SPANISH DESTROYED TENOCHTITLÁN AFTER CRUSHING THE AZTECS IN 1521. LAKE TEXCOCO WAS DRAINED, AND IN ITS PLACE ROSE THE CAPITAL OF NEW SPAIN—NOW MEXICO CITY, THE CAPITAL OF MEXICO.

By the end of the 1500s, there was almost no trace left of Tenochtitlán or its fabulous temple. The Spanish demolished all traces of the city, destroying all the figures of the gods and melting down the gold to take back to Europe. As the new city grew, the chances of finding any remains of the Aztec capital were remote. In 1914 a corner of the Great Temple was discovered. Workers building a new metro uncovered more of the temple in 1978, leading to a major archaeological investigation. This uncovered not only the entire temple site but many of the surrounding buildings.

LOOK CLOSER

According to a Franciscan friar who visited Tenochtitlán soon after the Spanish conquest, the central precinct contained not just the Templo Mayor but also another seventy-seven buildings.

▼ *A shrine from the Templo Mayor has been discovered in the center of Mexico City.*

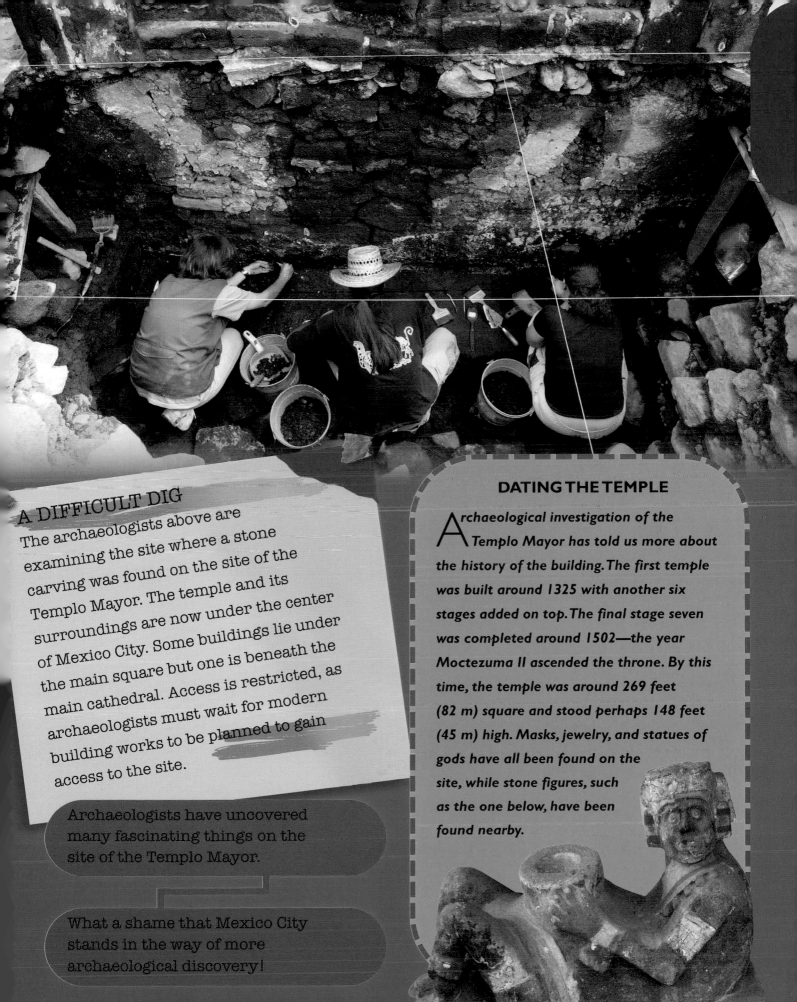

A DIFFICULT DIG

The archaeologists above are examining the site where a stone carving was found on the site of the Templo Mayor. The temple and its surroundings are now under the center of Mexico City. Some buildings lie under the main square but one is beneath the main cathedral. Access is restricted, as archaeologists must wait for modern building works to be planned to gain access to the site.

Archaeologists have uncovered many fascinating things on the site of the Templo Mayor.

What a shame that Mexico City stands in the way of more archaeological discovery!

DATING THE TEMPLE

Archaeological investigation of the Templo Mayor has told us more about the history of the building. The first temple was built around 1325 with another six stages added on top. The final stage seven was completed around 1502—the year Moctezuma II ascended the throne. By this time, the temple was around 269 feet (82 m) square and stood perhaps 148 feet (45 m) high. Masks, jewelry, and statues of gods have all been found on the site, while stone figures, such as the one below, have been found nearby.

MACHU PICCHU

Lost City
of the Incas

Location:
Peru, South America
Plateau at 7,710 feet (2,350 m)

WOW! Machu Picchu was a
country retreat for rich
Inca nobility.

THE ANDES MOUNTAINS

WERE ONCE HOME TO THE GREAT INCA EMPIRE. THE INCAS WERE A HIGHLY CIVILIZED PEOPLE WHO LEFT BEHIND HILLTOP TOWNS AND STORIES ABOUT THEIR VAST WEALTH.

THE INCAS

IN THE 1220s, MANCO CAPAC FOUNDED CUZCO IN THE PERUVIAN ANDES. DURING THE 1400s, THIS SMALL STATE GREW INTO THE MASSIVE INCA EMPIRE THAT STRETCHED DOWN THE PACIFIC COAST OF SOUTH AMERICA.

The Incas lived in the mountains but they were skilled farmers, building irrigated terraces along the steep slopes to grow crops to eat and feed to their animals. They kept llamas and alpacas as pack animals to carry their heavy loads and used their wool to make clothes and blankets to keep warm. They also built a vast road system that connected the outlying parts of the empire with Cuzco. Messengers ran along these roads carrying messages to and from the emperor and his regional governors.

THE INCA STATE

The Inca state was ruled by an all-powerful emperor—who was worshipped as the son of the Sun and carried in great state whenever he traveled around his empire. Alongside him were powerful nobles, who governed parts of the empire on his behalf. This figurine is made of silver and inlaid with gold, stone, and pink shell. It shows an idealized Inca man of high status. His earlobes are elongated by wearing large ear-discs, a practice restricted to the Inca nobility.

WRITING WITH STRING

The Incas never developed an alphabet to record information. Instead they used a quipu (left). A quipu consisted of a thick cord from which hung lengths of different colored string, each with many single, double, or triple knots tied into it. The color, length, and position of each hanging string on the cord and the type of knots it contained recorded information. This might be the population of a town, the amount of tax collected, or the size of the harvest. The scribe (right), who kept the quipus, was highly respected.

▼ The Incas built their streets with deep drains to carry rainwater into large storage tanks to be used for drinking, cooking, and irrigating the fields.

LOOK CLOSER

Although the Inca empire collapsed 500 years ago, many of the streets and walls survive in the cities of South America, as the Incas were such skilled builders and engineers.

The Incas built this drainage channel 500 years ago, and it survives today.

But what else built by the Incas still remains for people to see?

MACHU PICCHU

MACHU PICCHU LIES HIGH IN THE PERUVIAN ANDES, ABOUT **44** MILES (71 KM) NORTHWEST OF CUZCO. THIS TOWN IS NO ORDINARY PLACE.

Machu Picchu sits on a high saddle of land between two peaks that tower above the Urubamba Valley—the "sacred valley" of the Incas. The site was chosen by the Inca emperor Pachacuti Inca Yupanqui (reigned 1438–1471). The Incas believed that mountains and streams were the shrines or houses of their gods and spirits. The emperor built the town as a religious retreat for himself and his nobles, and a vantage point for the astronomer–priests.

INCA ASTRONOMY

The Incas observed the Sun, Moon, and stars, which they worshipped as gods and made detailed notes of their movements to keep their calendar. The royal astronomer–priests used Machu Picchu as a sacred observatory, although the precise details of what they did are unknown. Many large buildings face the winter solstice, when the Sun is lowest in the sky, and others face the summer solstice, when it is at its highest. Very few such buildings or monuments exist elsewhere, as the Spanish destroyed them when they conquered the Inca empire in the 1530s.

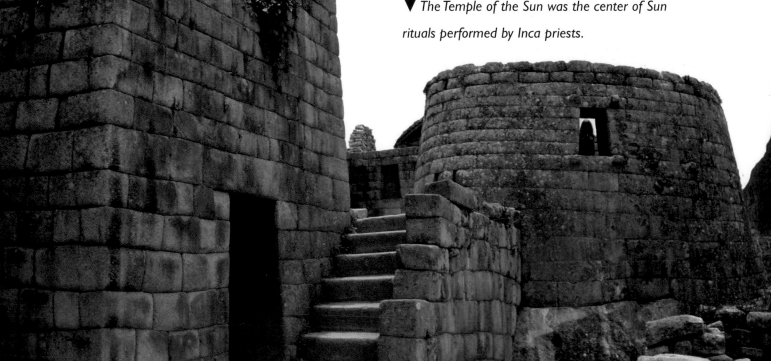

▼ *The Temple of the Sun was the center of Sun rituals performed by Inca priests.*

▼ The Intihuatana, or "Hitching Post of the Sun," is a large granite slab with geometric carvings. It was either used as a sundial or as an astronomical marker during important religious festivals.

Machu Picchu was obviously an important place, judging by its many splendid buildings.

Most people now think it was used as a place to worship the Sun, Moon, and stars.

One man, however, thought it was the lost city of the Incas and full of wealth!

LOOK CLOSER

The Incas were skilled stonemasons. Their strong walls have withstood earthquakes that have demolished many more recent buildings in the region.

▶ These stone houses would originally have had steep, thatched roofs, although these have collapsed and disintegrated over the years.

REDISCOVERY!

MACHU PICCHU IS ONE OF THE MOST CELEBRATED PLACES ON EARTH, BUT FOR CENTURIES IT LAY UNDISCOVERED IN THE JUNGLE.

By the time the Spanish arrived in Peru in 1532, Machu Picchu had been abandoned. The Spanish never found it, although local people continued to farm its terraced hillsides. In 1911, the American historian Hiram Bingham came to Peru in search of the lost city of Vilcabamba. An eleven-year-old guide named Agustín Lizárraga led him to a site covered with vegetation. Only when a survey team conducted a thorough investigation the next year did the scale of Machu Picchu become clear.

RESTORATION

When Bingham first visited Machu Picchu, it was covered up by jungle. Over the years, archaeologists have cleared the site and restored its many buildings. In 1981, the town and surrounding areas were declared an "historical sanctuary" of Peru. It is now a UNESCO World Heritage Site, allowing archaeologists to examine Machu Picchu in detail. However, pressure from tourism means that, like many other archaeological sites, Machu Picchu is now at great risk from human damage.

HIRAM BINGHAM

Hiram Bingham (1875–1956) was not a trained archaeologist but a historian. He first visited Peru in 1908 and returned in 1911 to find Vilcabamba. This was the last stronghold of the Incas until it was captured by the Spanish in 1572. It was rumored to be filled with rich treasures. Instead Bingham found Machu Picchu. He named it the Lost City of the Incas, the title of his book about the discovery, because he was convinced he had found the lost city of Vilcabamba. Bingham later became a keen pilot (he is seen on the far right of this picture), a U.S. senator, and a governor of Connecticut.

VILCABAMBA

It is always dangerous for archaeologists or historians to draw a conclusion without proper research or investigation, as Hiram Bingham found to his cost. In 1911, he set out to find the legendary city of Vilcabamba and believed, wrongly, that he found it at Machu Picchu. On his way back from Machu Picchu, Bingham found some more ruins but thought little of them. Only in 1964 did another American, Gene Savoy, realize that these ruins—known as Espíritu Pampa—were in fact the real Vilcabamba. Savoy's theory was confirmed by later research.

► The hillsides of Machu Picchu were terraced to grow enough food for the inhabitants, although the lack of warehouses suggests Machu Picchu was never intended to be a major trading center.

LOOK CLOSER

The stone houses were built on the terraces or in the courtyards. Most were one story high, but a few were taller—the upper story being reached by a rope ladder.

▲ Machu Picchu was never really lost. Local people knew about the ruins and two brothers farmed there, using the ancient walls as pens for their animals.

THE NORTHWEST COAST OF AMERICA IS RICH IN NATURAL RESOURCES. THE MAKAH PEOPLE DEVELOPED AN ADVANCED CULTURE BY EXPLOITING THE LAND, RIVERS, AND SEAS.

▲ *The Makah hunted whales until recent times. This photograph of their fishery on Tatoosh Island was taken around 1895.*

LIFE BY THE SEA

NATIVE AMERICANS ARE FAMED FOR THEIR ELABORATE WOOD CARVINGS AND BEAUTIFUL TEXTILES. THESE ARTIFACTS USUALLY PERISH WITH TIME, BUT TWO LUCKY FINDS HAVE REVEALED MUCH ABOUT THE MAKAH PEOPLE OF WASHINGTON STATE.

The Makah lived in Ozette for around 2,000 years, only abandoning the village in the 1930s. Ozette is situated on a sheltered bay next to the Pacific Ocean. In times of danger, its people escaped across a tidal causeway to the safety of a nearby island, which they also used to spot passing whales and fur seals. Over the years a large pile of midden built up on the island. Although well-preserved, its significance was not realized until storm waves undercut a bank on the mainland in 1970, revealing the remains of six wooden longhouses and their contents buried beneath a mudslide.

▲ *This beautifully decorated wooden model is of a Makah whaling canoe.*

LOOK CLOSER

Over the years the Makah people perfected the art of carving canoes out of solid trunks of wood and were skilled in using them to catch whales and other sea creatures.

▼ *Makah people fished humpback (below), grey, and sperm whales. One catch could supply an entire village with meat, oil, and bones.*

MAKING A LIVING

The Makah lived off the sea. They hunted fur seals, sea lions, and whales; fished deep water and inshore; and collected shellfish. This provided food, bones for making tools, and oil for cooking and lighting. They also caught elk and deer; trapped ducks, geese, and other seabirds; and ate wild berries and other forest plants. Forest cedarwood was used to build houses and make tools and weapons.

AN OZETTE LONGHOUSE

THE MAKAH PEOPLE TELL A STORY OF A MUDSLIDE SWEEPING INTO OZETTE MANY YEARS AGO, FLATTENING THE HOUSES AND BURYING THEIR INHABITANTS ALIVE.

In February 1970, six longhouses and their contents, as well as human skeletons, were discovered at Ozette. Thus the Makah people's story could be confirmed. Archaeologists have dated the buried longhouses to around 1500 A.D.

Three of the longhouses at Ozette have been fully excavated and studied by archaeologists. The thick mud that buried the wooden structures created the right oxygen-free conditions to preserve them and their contents, preventing any organic materials from decaying or rotting away. As a result, we now know what a Makah cedarwood longhouse looked like. A typical longhouse measured about 56 feet (17 m) long and 33 feet (10 m) wide and housed up to forty people from several related families.

BEACH ART

*T*he Makah people were highly skilled artists and craftworkers. Among the artifacts that archaeologists discovered was this unique cedarwood carving of a whale's fin. It is inlaid with more than 700 teeth from sea otters. Another find was a piece of cedarwood showing a carving of a whale outlined in white. The carving was probably made with a sharpened beaver's tooth. Cedar bark was used to make textiles such as sleeping mats, and it was woven into baskets for storage.

▶ *About six related families lived in the longhouse, each section of the house centered around a hearth. Each family had its own living area and a hearth for cooking.*

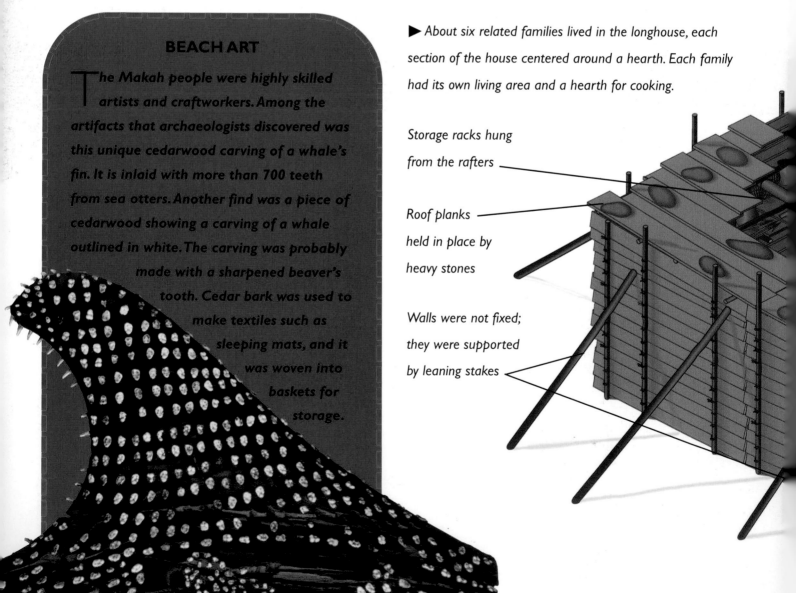

Storage racks hung from the rafters

Roof planks held in place by heavy stones

Walls were not fixed; they were supported by leaning stakes

Some archaeological finds are the result of chance, rather than a lengthy excavation.

If it were not for the storm in 1970, we would not even know about these longhouses!

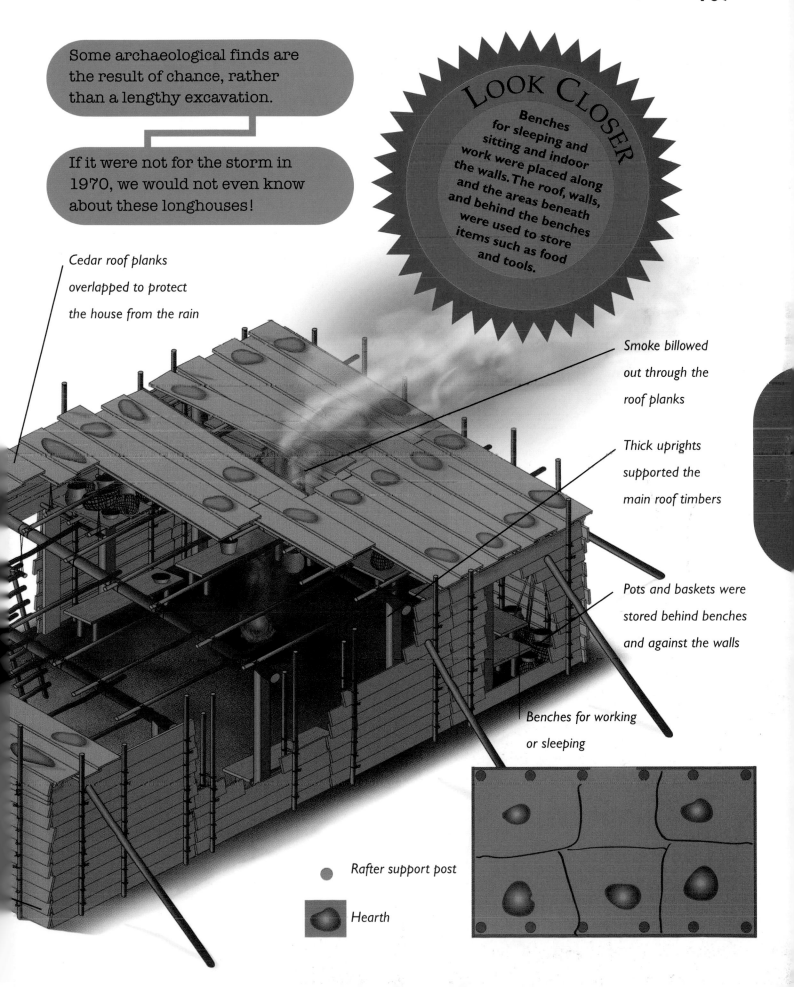

Cedar roof planks overlapped to protect the house from the rain

Smoke billowed out through the roof planks

Thick uprights supported the main roof timbers

Pots and baskets were stored behind benches and against the walls

Benches for working or sleeping

Rafter support post

Hearth

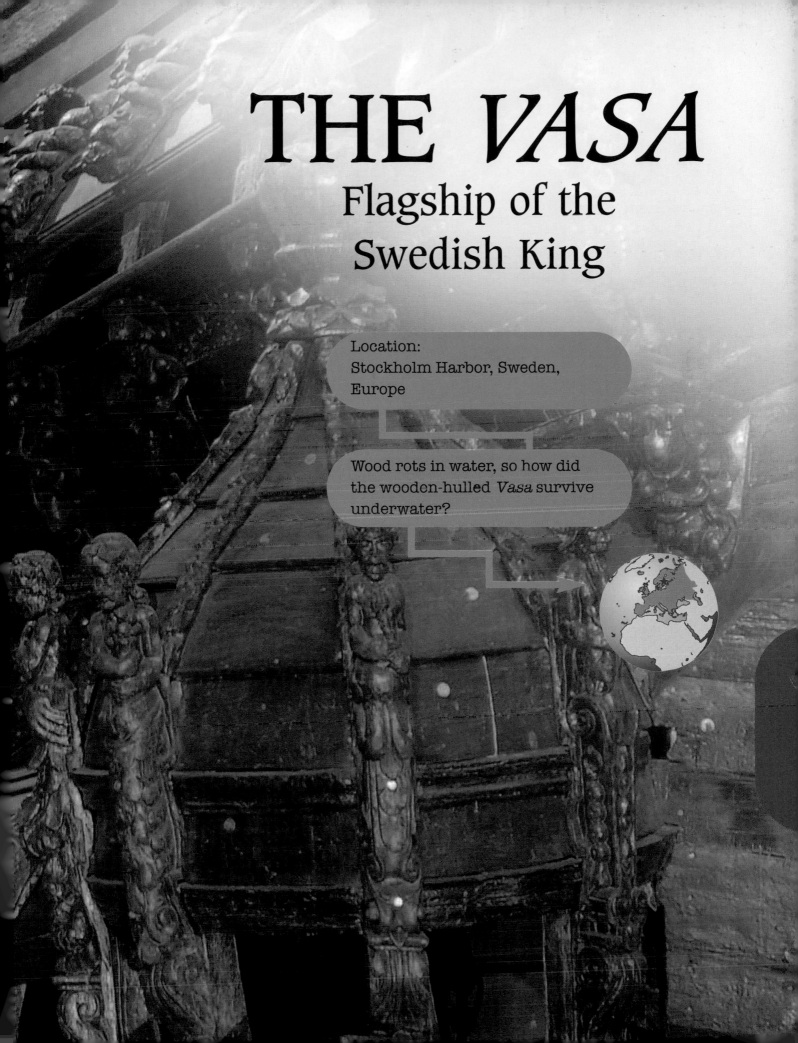

THE *VASA*
Flagship of the Swedish King

Location:
Stockholm Harbor, Sweden,
Europe

Wood rots in water, so how did
the wooden-hulled *Vasa* survive
underwater?

IN 1628, THE WORLD'S BIGGEST WARSHIP WAS LAUNCHED IN SWEDEN. THE *VASA* WAS THE FLAGSHIP OF THE NAVY AND WAS BUILT TO DEFEAT SWEDEN'S ENEMIES AROUND THE BALTIC SEA.

▲ The Vasa *was built and launched in Stockholm's harbor.*

KING'S FLAGSHIP

ON AUGUST 10, 1628, THE WARSHIP *VASA* SAILED OUT OF STOCKHOLM ON HER MAIDEN VOYAGE. THE SHIP WAS THE PRIDE OF THE SWEDISH NAVY. NO EXPENSE HAD BEEN SPARED IN EQUIPPING HER.

The *Vasa* was 226 feet (69 m) long and 38 feet (11.5 m) wide and weighed 1,210 tons. She was fitted with 64 guns, including 48 heavy cannons, and was decorated with many bright and elaborate sculptures. However, the ship's height and weight made her top-heavy. To counterbalance the ship, the designers loaded her keel with 124 tons of stone. The weather on her maiden voyage was calm, but a sudden squall of wind picked up as the ship was just 4,300 feet (1,310 m) from her berth. She keeled over to her port (left) side, and water flowed in through the open gun ports. The *Vasa* quickly sank, with the loss of at least thirty lives.

GUSTAVUS II ADOLPHUS

Sweden's greatest king, Gustavus II Adolphus (right), ruled from 1611 to 1632. With his powerful armed forces, he waged successful wars against Denmark, Russia, and Poland, gaining territory around the Baltic Sea. Gustavus was a devout Protestant. In 1630, he helped the Protestants fight against the Catholic Habsburgs in the Thirty Years' War in Germany. Gustavus lost his life at the Battle of Lützen in 1632.

The *Vasa* was designed to be the biggest and most powerful warship of the time.

Surely the ship's designers would have made certain that the vessel would float?

▶ *Flagship of Gustavus's navy, the* Vasa *was a three-masted warship.*

RAISING THE VASA

THE VASA SANK IN 105 FEET (32 M) OF WATER JUST 394 FEET (120 M) OFF SHORE. IN 1664, A PRIMITIVE DIVING BELL WAS USED TO RECOVER SOME OF THE SHIP'S CANNON.

In 1956 divers rediscovered the Vasa sitting upright on the seabed. Five years later, the ship was lifted off the seabed by placing six steel cables under her hull and attaching the cable ends to a pair of lifting pontoons. She was then carried into shallower water. There, the gun ports were closed, and the holes where the iron bolts used to build the ship had rusted away were plugged to make the ship watertight for the final lift. On April 24, 1961, she was finally raised to the surface and placed in a dry dock for restoration.

The Vasa was built of oak timbers and carried sculptures of pine and linden wood.

But wood rots in water, and the Vasa has been resting on the seabed for more than 330 years.

So how come so much of the ship has survived under the water through all this time?

▼ The Vasa was first placed in a dry dock (below) and was later transferred to a purpose-built museum in Stockholm. Today, the Vasa is Sweden's top tourist attraction.

PRESERVING THE *VASA*

The main danger in restoring the ship's hull was that it would dry out and disintegrate once out of the water. The wood was therefore sprayed for seventeen years with polyethylene glycol (PEG), a waxy chemical that has replaced the water inside the timbers. However, this produces a build-up of sulphuric acid, making the wood brittle and prone to decay. As it does so, the braces that support the ship press deeper into the hull each year. Conservation experts are currently investigating how to stabilize the wood and thus save the ship.

◀ Some of the sculptures have survived almost intact.

▲ The Vasa is decorated with 500 wooden sculptures.

LOOK CLOSER

Most submerged wood is eaten by the shipworm, so there are few old wooden ships still afloat. But shipworm cannot survive in the cold, salty Baltic, so the Vasa is almost intact.

THE MARY ROSE

In 1545, the English warship **Mary Rose** keeled over in a gust of wind and sank when water poured through the gun ports. The ship was brought to the surface in 1982 and, like the Vasa, placed in a dry dock and treated with polyethylene glycol. Unlike the Vasa, however, one side of the hull had been eaten by shipworm. The other side was buried in the mud and thus escaped destruction.

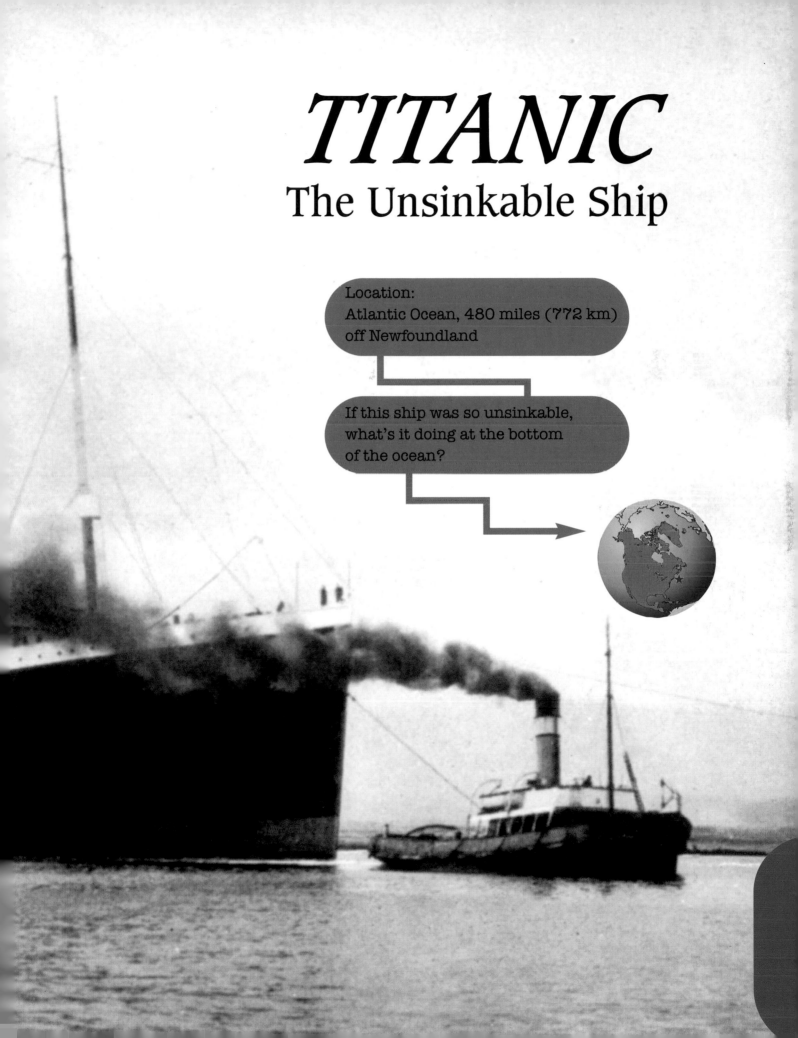

TITANIC
The Unsinkable Ship

Location:
Atlantic Ocean, 480 miles (772 km)
off Newfoundland

If this ship was so unsinkable,
what's it doing at the bottom
of the ocean?

WHEN THE **LUXURIOUS** STEAMSHIP RMS *TITANIC* WAS LAUNCHED IN 1911, IT WAS SAID TO BE **UNSINKABLE.** ON APRIL 10, 1912, IT BEGAN ITS MAIDEN VOYAGE ACROSS THE ATLANTIC OCEAN.

LUXURY LINER

THE *TITANIC* WAS BUILT TO ACCOMMODATE 1,324 PASSENGERS, OF WHOM 329 WERE TRAVELING FIRST CLASS IN THE TOP FOUR DECKS OF THE SHIP.

No expense was spared in making RMS *Titanic* the most luxurious ship in the world. Everything on board was brand new, and most of it had been designed specially for the ship. The public rooms were filled with grand furniture and connected by sweeping staircases and wide promenades. Even the second- and third-class (steerage) quarters—the latter filled mainly with emigrants to America—were well equipped by most standards. Almost 900 crew were on hand to look after the needs of all the passengers.

▼ *A group of shipyard workers gathers under the huge bronze propellers of RMS Titanic, giving an idea of the ship's vast size.*

LOOK CLOSER

The ship's hull was divided into sixteen compartments separated by watertight bulkheads. The bulkheads only reached 10 feet (3 m) above the waterline, so water could spill over them.

▲ The reading room was a favorite retreat for first-class women passengers, as they were forbidden to join men in the smoking room.

LIFE ON BOARD

Whatever the class of travel, life on board the Titanic was first-rate. The open decks and covered promenades on the ship allowed passengers to get plenty of exercise and fresh air. Below decks, first-class passengers could exercise in the gym, play squash, swim in the pool, or enjoy a Turkish bath. A range of restaurants, lounges, bars, smoking rooms, and hairdressers catered to their every need. Second- and third-class passengers had their own facilities. Families and single women slept in cabins, while third-class single male passengers slept together in a huge dormitory in the bow.

FINDING THE *TITANIC*

EVERYONE KNOWS THE *TITANIC* SANK IN THE NORTH ATLANTIC, SOMEWHERE EAST OF CANADA. BUT WHERE EXACTLY WAS THE SHIP?

Even a few years ago it would have been impossible to locate a ship sunk deep in the ocean. But after the end of World War II in 1945, French and American scientists pioneered the exploration of the world's oceans. New technology such as submersibles and sonar (a communication and position-finding device) meant that by 1980 all the ocean floors were mapped. Wherever the *Titanic*'s wreck lay, scientists now had the technology to find it.

Close reading of the reports about the sinking compiled soon after the event located the ship about 480 miles (772 km) off Newfoundland. The Atlantic seabed shelves deeply here, so the *Titanic* was probably lying in about 12,470 feet (3,800 m) of water.

LOOK CLOSER

Many wooden ships have perished underwater. The *Titanic* was built of metals, which corroded slowly in the cold ocean waters. The bow, though rusty, is still recognizable.

THE DISCOVERY TEAM

The team that discovered the *Titanic* was working on a joint French/American project. On September 1, 1985, Dr. Robert Ballard was in charge of the surface ship trying to find the *Titanic*'s location. Cameras on a submersible controlled from the ship spotted one of the *Titanic*'s boilers. In 1986, Ballard and two others visited the site in a submersible and photographed it. They were the first people to see the famous ship for seventy-three years.

▲ *Dr. Robert Ballard shows a plan of the* Titanic.
He discovered the ship's watery grave in 1985.

At the bottom of the ocean, where the *Titanic*'s wreck lies, it is pitch black.

The temperature is nearly freezing; no more than an icy 36°F. Brr!!

No human could survive without the protection of a submersible.

SUBMERSIBLES

Submersibles allow humans to live and work deep under water. Some are controlled from a ship on the surface, while others have crew on board. Ballard and his team used both kinds. These small submarines are strong enough to withstand the massive pressure caused by the water above them but maneuverable enough to be navigated around the ocean floor. Sonar navigation and strong lights mean they can observe a sunken ship at close range.

THE *TITANIC* TODAY

S OME 80 YEARS AFTER THE SHIP SANK, THE *TITANIC* CONTINUES TO ATTRACT PROFESSIONAL INTEREST. MARINE ARCHAEOLOGISTS HAVE LEARNED MUCH FROM THE CONDITION OF THE WRECK AND HAVE WORKED OUT EXACTLY WHY THE SHIP SANK.

The initial discovery of the hull in two pieces confirmed that the ship broke up as it sank. However, the real reason why it sank has only recently become known. Since the hull is buried under 574 feet (175 m) of mud, archaeologists have only been able to examine the hull using sonar. This revealed that the iceberg made six narrow incisions in the hull. Since these incisions were in different compartments, water flooded much of the hull and slowly caused it to sink.

The ship struck an iceberg on the night of April 14 and finally sank on April 15.

Some people escaped in lifeboats, but there were not enough for all on board.

The ship sank with the loss of about 1,517 people; the exact number has not been confirmed.

▼ *Rows of dinner plates and many other objects can be found on the ocean floor near the wreckage.*

WHAT NEXT FOR THE SHIP?

Ever since the *Titanic* sank, plans have been put forward to raise it from the sea floor. However, the *Titanic* sank in such deep water that it would have been impossible to raise it at the time. The hull has now deteriorated so much in the salty water that what is left of it would break up if it was moved. More importantly, the ship is an official wreck site and the burial place for more than 1,500 people. Many people argue that the ship and its remains should be left in peace. While interest in the *Titanic* continues to rage, the debate about its future remains controversial.

THE *TITANIC* LIVES ON

The Titanic has fascinated people ever since it sank in 1912. Countless books have been written about the ship, while its story has also been turned into several musicals and films. The most recent film—Titanic (1997), starring Leonardo DiCaprio and Kate Winslet (above)—won eleven Academy Awards, including Oscars® for Best Picture and Best Director.

EXAMINING THE REMAINS

While it is interesting to look at the original dinner plates used in the first-class dining rooms (right), or examine the many other artifacts that have been salvaged from the wreckage, the real excitement lies in the scientific investigation of the hull. Archaeologists have discovered that the steel used to build the ship had become brittle through exposure to low water temperatures. On the night the ship sank, the water temperature was only about 32°F (0°C). The steel also had a high sulphur content, which made it more liable to fracture. These two factors may explain why the iceberg inflicted such severe damage when the ship hit it.

PLACES TO VISIT

The Americas are packed full of archaeological sites and remains which tell us much about our history and who has lived here before us. Many of these sites are open to the public and are well worth a visit. Some even encourage volunteers to help with excavations: who knows— you might even uncover some archaeological secrets of your own!

AMERICA DINOSAUR PARK

Late Jurassic Period
(over 140 million years ago)
Location: Themopolis, Wyoming
Type of Site: Dinosaur remains
■ Dinosaur bones were first discovered at Warm Springs Ranch in 1993 where there are over 60 identified dinosaur dig sites in a 500-acre area. The Big Horn Basin Foundation is an educational organization offering amateurs the chance to dig with paleontologists and perhaps uncover some real dinosaur bones.
www.wyodino.org/

RAVEN SITE

1000 C.E.
Location: Colorado River
Type of Site: Prehistoric settlement
■ The ruins of this prehistoric city were donated to The Archaeological Conservancy in 2003 and this area is now part of an ongoing research project. The site, which overlooks the Little Colorado River, holds many cultural features of the Mogollon and Anasazi people, and the museum on site showcases many of these artifacts.
www.wmonline.com/ATTRACT/raven.htm

TREASURES OF THE FOUR CORNERS

500 C.E.
Location: Colorado
Type of Site: Anasazi Heritage Center
■ The Heritage Center houses a collection of almost two million archaeological artifacts, documents and samples, which offer a valuable insight into how and where the Anasazi people lived.
www.blm.gov/co/st/en/fo/ahc.html

MESA VERDE NATIONAL PARK

450 – 1300 C.E.
Location: Colorado
Type of Site: Cliff Dwellings of the Anasazi tribe
■ Anasazi culture flourished for hundreds of years at this site. The remains are now part of the national park, and wandering among these once-thriving settlements will transport you to another world.
www.nps.gov/archive/meve/home.htm

TONTO NATIONAL MONUMENT

1050 – 1450 C.E.
Location: Southeastern Arizona
Type of Site: Salado settlement
■ Archaeologists uncovered various dwellings built into the cliff face that are thought to be the remains of the Salado settlement. The Salado people made their living from the mountainous terrain in the region and pottery pieces, and beautiful woven fabrics have been found at the site.
www.go-arizona.com/Tonto-National-Monument-Attractions

CHACO CULTURE NATIONAL PARK

850 C.E.

Location: El Morro,
New Mexico

Type of Site: Chaco settlement

■ The Chacoan people built magnificent public and ceremonial buildings in the Canyon of El Morro —the largest building is estimated to have contained over 600 rooms, and the remains have taught us much about the culture of the clans and people who settled here. The national park museum also has many artifacts on display from this period.
www.nps.gov/history/museum/ exhibits/chcu/

THE GAULT SITE

12,000 B.C.

Location: Central Texas

Type of Site: Clovis Cultural Site

■ The people who once settled here were hunters and gatherers who made use of the flint commonly found in the area to make weapons such as spear points. Archaeologists have found Clovis weaponry gathered in piles, thought to be stashes hidden by the Clovis people.
www.texasbeyondhistory.net/gault/ index.html

POVERTY POINT NATIONAL MONUMENT

1650–700 B.C.

Location: Northeastern Louisiana

Type of Site: Prehistoric earthworks

■ Manmade earth mounds can be found dating back to the first and second millennia B.C. at this state-run park. It is estimated that it took the inhabitants of Poverty Point five million hours of labor to build the massive earthworks. Perhaps the most famous of these is the enormous mound, shaped like a bird with outstretched wings. The visitor center also has a diverse collection of artifacts uncovered from this area.
www.nps.gov/popo/

CENTRAL AMERICA TIKAL

Fourth century B.C.

Location: Guatemala

Type of Site: Ancient ruins of the Maya Civilization

■ This Mayan society thrived for almost 1,000 years with an estimated population of 100,000. Archaeologists have discovered traces of many of their accomplishments from the arts to astronomy, and today Tikal is one of Guatemala's top tourist attractions.
www.destination360.com/tikal.htm

CARIBBEAN TIBES INDIGENOUS CEREMONIAL CENTER

25 C.E.

Location: Ponce, Puerto Rico

Type of Site: Indigenous site of the Igneri and Tainos tribes

■ This site represents the population of indigenous people who inhabited the area more than 1,000 years before Columbus encountered the New World. The ceremonial center has around 80,000 visitors each year, and is an important connection to the indigenous culture and society of this region.
www.ponce.inter.edu/tibes/ tibes.html

CANADA

Eighteenth century

Location: Nova Scotia

Type of Site: French Fortress

■ The Fortress of Louisbourg was built by the French to protect their interest in the fishing port of Cape Breton Island in a struggle with Great Britain for colonial supremacy in North America. The fortress has since been reconstructed and is the main attraction at the national historic park, which offers a unique insight into 1700's colonial history.
www.louisbourg.ca/fort/

GLOSSARY

■ **A.D.**
Anno Domini: in the year of our Lord. 1 A.D. is equivalent to one year after Christ's birth.

■ **AMPHITHEATER**
Large Roman stadium where audiences watched gladiator fights and sporting events

■ **AMPHORA**
Large, two-handled pottery jar with a pointed end used to transport wine, olive oil, and other liquids around the Mediterranean world

■ **AQUEDUCT**
Pipe or covered channel carrying water

■ **ARCHAEOLOGY**
Study of the past carried out by archaeologists using excavation, examination, and analysis of material remains

■ **ARTIFACT**
Object made or used by humans

■ **B.C.**
Before Christ: a religious system of dating in which B.C. is equivalent to one year before Christ's birth

■ **C.**
circa, the Latin for "about"; used before a date when the actual date is not known

■ **CARBON DATING**
Scientific technique used to date organic or living matter, such as bones, wood, and skin, by measuring the decay of its carbon isotopes (atoms); also called radiocarbon dating

■ **CARTOUCHE**
Oval frame with two long, straight sides used in ancient Egypt to enclose the hieroglyphs that spelled out a royal name

■ **CELTS**
Ancient people who lived in central and western Europe from around 500 B.C. until 600 A.D., surviving for much longer in some western areas

■ **CHARCOAL**
A form of carbon made by burning organic matter such as wood in the absence of air

■ **CIVILIZATION**
Highly advanced society

■ **CODEX**
An ancient manuscript made in the form of a book rather than rolled up into a scroll

■ **CT SCAN**
Computerized tomography scan: scientific technique originally developed for medicine that uses both X-rays and computer enhancement to produce cross sections of the whole body; the technique enables archaeologists to look inside a mummy without removing its wrappings

■ **DIG**
Archaeological excavation

■ **DUGOUT**
Canoe or other boat carved out of a solid tree trunk or large branch

■ **EXCAVATION**
The process of digging up a site to find archaeological evidence

■ **FLAGSHIP**
Most important ship in a fleet; often the one from which the commander issues orders to the rest of the fleet

■ **FLINT**
Hard stone used to make prehistoric tools and weapons

■ **FORUM**
Large open space in the middle of a Roman town used for public meetings and events

■ **FRESCO**
Watercolor painting on a wall or ceiling completed before the plaster dries

■ **GRAVE GOODS**
Objects such as craft work, food, weapons, jewelry, and pieces of furniture that are buried in the grave with the body as offerings to the gods or so that the deceased can use them in the afterlife

■ **HIEROGLYPHS**
Writing system using symbols instead of letters

■ **HILL FORT**
Fortress or fortification on a hilltop; the hill fort consists of rings of earth walls and ditches, sometimes reinforced with stone or wood, inside which the occupants could shelter in times of danger

■ **HULL**
Main body of a ship

■ **ICE AGE**
Period of time when the world was much colder and ice covered much of the land

■ **IRON AGE**
Period of time when people learned to make tools and weapons in iron; in Europe, from around 1000 B.C. until Roman times

■ **LABYRINTH**
Complex network of chambers, paths, and tunnels

■ **LEGEND**
Traditional story that is not supported by any historical evidence

■ **MIDDEN**
Heap of ancient rubbish close to a house or inhabited area

■ **MINOTAUR**
Legendary monster with the head of a bull and the body of a man; supposed to have lived in the labyrinth in Knossos

■ **MOSAIC**
Picture or design made from small fragments of colored stone or glass

■ **MUMMY**
The preserved remains of a human or animal body

■ **MURAL**
Large painting or picture on a wall

■ **NEOLITHIC**
Belonging to the New Stone Age, a period from about 8000 B.C. in the Near East to around 2000 B.C. in northwest Europe.

■ ORGANIC MATERIALS
Substances such as bone, hide, horn, ivory, or wood that were once part of a living organism

■ PALAEOLITHIC
Belonging to the Old Stone Age, a very long period of time stretching from about 2.5 million years ago to around 9000 B.C.

■ PHARAOH
Ancient Egyptian king

■ PIGMENT
Powder sometimes mixed with a liquid such as water to make paint

■ POLYETHYLENE GLYCOL (PEG)
Waxy substance sprayed on wet timber to replace the water in the wood and thus preserve the wood as it dries out in the air

■ PREHISTORY
Time before written records were kept; this period varies around the world as different cultures developed writing systems at different times

■ QUIPU
Elaborate knotted strings used to keep records by the Incas of the Peruvian Andes

■ SARCOPHAGUS
Stone or marble coffin or tomb, often bearing carvings or inscriptions, in which the corpse is placed

■ SEAL
Small clay, ivory, metal, stone, or wood block bearing an engraving, which is stamped onto wet clay or molten wax to mark official documents or traded goods to indicate authority or authorship; in Mesopotamia, seals were often cylindrical and rolled across the clay

■ SONAR
Acronym for SOund NAvigation and Ranging, a communication and position-ranging device used in underwater navigation and investigation

■ STRATIGRAPHY
Study of the formation, composition, and sequence (order) of strata (layers of remains), a technique used by archaeologists to help them work out the timescale and order of events of the site under investigation

■ SUBMERSIBLE
Submarine capable of descending to great depths; submersibles can be manned or remotely controlled from a surface ship and usually carry powerful lights, sonar, and other equipment to navigate through the murky waters and locate a sunken ship or other wreckage

■ TERRACOTTA
A baked form of clay used to make ornaments and statues

■ VILLA
Large country house

■ WHEELER SYSTEM
Excavation of a site in a pattern of regular squares or rectangles, leaving gaps between them; named after British archaeologist Sir Mortimer Wheeler, who developed the system

FURTHER READING

THE ANCIENT CITY
by Peter Connolly (OUP, 2001)

ARCHAEOLOGY: A VERY SHORT INTRODUCTION
by Paul Bahn (OUP, 1996)

AWESOME ARCHAEOLOGY
by Nick Arnold (Scholastic, 2001)

EYEWITNESS ARCHAEOLOGY
by Jane McIntosh (Dorling Kindersley, 1994)

KINGFISHER KNOWLEDGE: LIFE IN ANCIENT ROME
by Simon Adams (Kingfisher, 2005)

WEB SITES

Ask an adult to help you find additional web sites and check them out before you use them.

BBC archaeology web site:
www.bbc.co.uk/history/archaeology

Channel 4's *Time Team* web site:
www.channel4.com/history/timeteam/index.html

Archaeological site for children:
www.digonsite.com

Directory of highly readable articles about archaeology:
http://dmoz.org/Kids_and_Teens/School_Time/ Social_Studies/Archaeology/

Young Archaeologists Club:
www.britarch.ac.uk/yac/index.html

Latest archaeological news:
www.sciencedaily.com/news/fossils_ruins/archaeology

INDEX

ACKNOWLEDGMENTS

AKG Images: 10, 29t, 54/55, 65t Johann Brandste 11t; Cameraphoto 59b; Peter Connolly 5 (1900 B.C.E.), 27t; Erich Lessing 5 (520 B.C.E.), 11cr, 46/47, 51, 52, 53t, 84t; Nimatallah 19t; **Alamy:** Content Mine Information 57; Danita Delimont 60b; David Hilbert 61t; Peter Horree 56; Pictorial Press 24/25; Robert Harding Picture Library 25; Visual Arts Library (London) 60t; **Ancient Art and Architecture Collection:** 12, 67t; **Art Archive:** Gianni Dagli Orti 75b; Cornelis De Vries 111b; Egyptian Museum Cairo/Alfredo Dagli 73l; Musée du Château de Versailles/Gianni Dagli Orti 111t; Musee du Louvre Paris/Gianni Dagli Orti 77b; Museo Giudad Mexico/Gianni Dagli 90; Museo Naval Madrid/Gianni Dagli Orti 50/51; **Bridgeman Art Library:** British Museum, London, UK, Photo © Boltin Picture Library 77t; **Corbis:** 19b, 116; Paul Almasy 21b; Daniel Aquiler/Reuters 93t; Bettmann 82, 84b, 100b; Kristi J. Black 69b; Jonathan Blair 61b; Sheldon Collins 6/7; Richard A. Cooke 106; Macduff Everton 113t; Mario Guzmanlepa 7l; Peter Harholdt 105t; Jason Hawkes 49b; Jon Hicks 110; Jeremy Horner 97b; Huntingdon Brothers 104 Wolfgang Kaehler 29b; Charles and Josette Lenars 21t, 93b; Diego Lezama 18/19; Joe Marquette 119t; Jose Manuel Sanchis Calvete 13b; Sean Sexton Collection 85b; Keren Su 68; The Gallery Collection 13t; Underwood & Underwood 117t; John Van Hasselt 100t; Ralph White 118, 119b, 120, 121b; Roger Wood 26; **Getty Images:** David Savill 37b; **Kobal Collection:** Warner Bros/Alex Bailey 27b; Mary Evans Picture Library: 24, 35b, 74, 89b, 117b; Edwin Wallace 35t; Musee de Chantillonnais, Chantillon Sur Seine, Cote D'Or, France: 53b; **Photodisc:** 83b; Photos.com: 5 (12,000 B.C.E.); 5 (1322 B.C.E.); 5 (290 B.C.E.); 83t, 86/87, 92; Rex Features: Sipa Press 69t; **Science Photo Library:** Adam Hart-Davis 113b; James King-Holmes 15t; Alexander Tsiaras 6; **Shutterstock:** 6 (1440); Albo 6 (1628), 108/109; Carlos Arguelles 101t; Brett Atkins 105b; Konstantin Baskakov 40; Natalia Bratsalvsky 6 (1450s); Bryan Busovicki 94/95; Diane Cramer 6 (79 C.E.), 80; Jack Cronkhite 62/63; Dainis Derics 70/71; Emily Goodwin 5 (1700 B.C.E.), 30/31; Vladimir Korostyshevskiy 6 (196 B.C.E.), 75t; Grigory Kubatyan 6 (79 C.E.); Jon Naustdalslid 65b; Mikhail Nekrasov 78/79; Monika Olszewska 41, 42/43; Adrian Phillips 99b, 101b; Svetlana Privezentseva 40/041; Scott Robinson 43b; Stephen Strathdee 102/103; Yan Vugenfiver 66l; Ke Wang 5 (210 B.C.E.); Lynn Watson 73r; Richard Welter 91b; **Topham:** 5 (2600 B.C.E.); 6 (1912); 15b, 16/17, 20, 21c, 33b, 33t, 36, 59t, 67b, 112, 114/115; Alinari 7r, 98; Ashmolean Museum 44; Fotoarchives 91t; KPA 121t; Photonews 45; Print Collector/HIP 28; Roger-Viollet 8/9 11cl, 37t; Charles Walker 32; World History Archive 22/23, 34/35, 38/39; **Vasa Museum:** National Maritime Museums, Sweden 113c; **Werner Forman Archives:** 81b, 81t, 89t; British Museum 48; Egyptian Museum Cairo 43t, 58, 72; Museo Archeologico Nazionale, Naples, Italy 85t; Museo Nazionale Preistorico Etnografico Luigi Pigorini, Rome 88; Museum fur Volkerkunde, Berlin 96, 97t; Narodni Museum, Prague 49t; N.J. Saunders 97c, 99t; C.E. Strouhal 43c; **Wikimedia Commons:** 14.

CONSULTANT: DR. PAUL G. BAHN
PROJECT EDITOR: ANNE O'DALY
LAYOUT EDITOR: LEON GRAY
DESIGNER: LISA ROBB
DESIGN MANAGER: SARAH WILLIAMS
PICTURE RESEARCHER: LAILA TORSUN